ID975254

FRANK

FRANK
Fighting Back

Frank Bruno with Kevin Mitchell

RICHMOND PUBLIC LIBRARY CALIFORNIA 94804

YELLOW JERSEY PRESS

LONDON

31143007452742
B BRUNO, F.
Bruno, Frank.
Frank : fighting back

Published by Yellow Jersey Press 2005

2 4 6 8 10 9 7 5 3 1

Copyright © Hamlet Advertising Limited 2005

Frank Bruno has asserted his right under the Copyright, Designs
and Patents Act 1988 to be identified as the author of this work

This book is sold subject to the condition that it shall not, by way of trade
or otherwise, be lent, resold, hired out, or otherwise circulated without the
publisher's prior consent in any form of binding or cover other than that
in which it is published and without a similar condition including this
condition being imposed on the subsequent purchaser

First published in Great Britain in 2005 by
Yellow Jersey Press

Yellow Jersey Press
Random House, 20 Vauxhall Bridge Road,
London SW1V 2SA

Random House Australia (Pty) Limited
20 Alfred Street, Milsons Point, Sydney,
New South Wales 2061, Australia

Random House New Zealand Limited
18 Poland Road, Glenfield,
Auckland 10, New Zealand

Random House (Pty) Limited
Isle of Houghton, Corner Boundary Road & Carse O'Gowrie,
Houghton, 2198, South Africa

The Random House Group Limited Reg. No. 954009
www.randomhouse.co.uk

A CIP catalogue record for this book
is available from the British Library

ISBN 0–224–07776–7

Papers used by Random House are natural, recyclable products made from
wood grown in sustainable forests. The manufacturing processes conform to
the environmental regulations of the country of origin

Typeset by Palimpsest Book Production Limited, Polmont, Stirlingshire
Printed and bound in Great Britain by Clays Ltd, St Ives plc

To Laura and the kids . . . and to George

Contents

Introduction

MY NAME IS FRANK BRUNO. YOU PROBABLY KNOW ME AS A FIGHTER, the happy guy on the telly with the one-liners, the big guy in panto. Maybe you were there the night I won the world title. Maybe you shouted 'Broo-no!' at one of my fights. I was public property, a celebrity they say. And there wasn't much people didn't know about my life, about my wife and kids, the big house in the country, the MBE and all the other trappings. Strangers said hello in the street. They still do. But one Monday in September 2003 I discovered another Frank Bruno – someone even I didn't know.

That was the day I was admitted to a mental hospital. They told me I was a danger to myself and to others. Sectioned, they call it. Banged up. I'd been troubled since I retired. I quit boxing after I lost my title in 1996, and things went seriously wrong in the years after, but I had no idea I was so ill. If I didn't know, who did? Only those very close to me. Without them, I hate to think what would have happened.

When I came out, I had to get to know the new me, the new Bruno. It isn't easy. You have to like yourself, but you have to recognise your faults. I've made mistakes in life – everyone has – and I'll probably make more. But I hope they'll be honest ones.

Most of my life I've been told what to do: in reform school, on the building site, in the gym, on the stage. But in the hospital at Goodmayes, they asked me what I wanted to do. They taught me to be responsible for my actions. They brought order into my life where there had been chaos. When I went in there, I was in a bad way, I'd been mixing with the wrong people, doing drugs, acting weird. I know I have to put my past behind me. I'm forty-three and free. If I want to stay that way, it's up to me.

For all my problems, I've been lucky in life. I got four shots at the world title before I won it. I made a lot of money and a lot of friends. I haven't lost my sense of humour – it's what helped me through my ordeal. I've had laughs from Bogotá to Vegas, and I've got three wonderful kids. I want one more favour from life: I want you to understand what I went through. It's important not just to me but to mentally ill people everywhere, people not as lucky as me, who never get better. And, in case you think it only happens to other people, it might be important to you.

I

The Worst Day of My Life

THE FIRST DAY OF THE WORST MONTH OF MY LIFE STARTED
like many others. As best I can, I'll try to piece it together.
Sometimes I can recall that day – Monday, 22 September
2003 – as if it were yesterday. But mostly it's a blur.

I woke up early at my house at Stondon Massey in the
Essex countryside, had some breakfast and got ready to go
into London. I had to be at the children's hospital in Great
Ormond Street at eleven o'clock. It was one of the jobs I
always looked forward to, talking to kids. But I was in no
condition to help anyone. I was the one who needed help.

It was my eldest daughter, Nicola, who knew something
was up. She was staying with me because I'd been behaving
strangely for some time. But Nicola saw something was very
wrong that morning, worse than my midnight drives across
London, worse than my buying sprees and the late-night
phone calls.

Over the previous few months, I had still been getting out

3

and about to boxing shows. It would have been better if I'd stayed at home. People were shocked when they saw me. I was seriously underweight. I probably hadn't been so skinny since I was a teenager. Friends were whispering behind my back that I looked ill. They'd heard the rumours. How I'd turned up in Blackpool one night, wandering the streets in the early hours. How I had been directing traffic outside my house. How I'd bought a boxing ring and been sleeping in it. I'd even told Harry Carpenter how sexy he looked without his glasses. God knows what his wife Phyllis thought of that.

I was DJing up and down the country at various clubs, bits and pieces here and there, and the money was rolling in. What I did know was that work was a release. I was exhausting myself on purpose, trying to wear myself out so my mind would slow down.

My problems had been building up for years, but I wasn't aware of how bad things were at first. It all started when I lost to Mike Tyson in March of 1996. He took the world title I had won only six months before; I'd hardly had a chance to enjoy it. In 1998 a psychiatrist told me I had a bipolar affective disorder, what used to be called manic depression. Then my marriage to Laura broke down and one of my best friends committed suicide. I felt like I was turning into a different person, someone I didn't know – or like. Here I was, living in a big house on my own, not knowing who my real friends were any more . . . the whole show had just exploded, and the pressure was building up by the day.

I told myself it would pass, that I'd calm down eventually. But there was another voice inside trying to tell me different.

Trying to tell me the truth. And I know now that the truth can give you the hardest blow of all if you don't face up to it.

As a boxer, I was used to deceiving myself. We spend most of our careers pretending, telling little white lies. You have to do it in the ring because you don't want your opponent to know if you're hurt or tired. You have to do it outside the ring when your manager shows you a deal you don't like. Most of my life I've been in a goldfish bowl – twenty-four hours a day, 365 days a year, you have to live up to an image someone else has created for you. My image had always been the happy-go-lucky joker. I found it hard to think of myself as mentally ill.

That spring, my sister Joan moved in to keep an eye on me. 'You need help, Franklin,' she said. I wouldn't listen. But she did get me to see a doctor. She even persuaded me to go to the Priory in Essex but I came home after one night. I didn't see how it could help me.

For about a month before they came to take me away, nurses and doctors from the hospital nearby were calling at my home to check up on me. Laura and the kids had moved out long ago and our house seemed as cold as a dentist's waiting room. I know the doctors were trying to help but, to me, these were strangers invading my private space. All the security cameras at the gate and locks on the door couldn't keep them out. And I didn't want to listen to any of their advice.

I knew it had to stop, though. I couldn't keep track of time or what was going on around me. I wasn't making any sense in conversations. I turned up at one DJing gig looking so awful and rambled on so much people thought I was crazy. In a way, of course, I was. Three days before my world caved in, I was having my picture taken with Sooty. How weird can life get? I'm slowly losing a grip on reality and I've got my hand up a puppet's backside promoting a Christmas pantomime.

'Dad, you're acting really strangely now,' Nicola said that Monday morning. 'Are you OK?'

'Don't worry, Nick. I'm fine,' I said. But I was talking gibberish and Nicola was frightened for me. Maybe even frightened *of* me, as well.

'Dad, you're not going into London. I think you should see a doctor. Now. You've got to go to the hospital, Dad. I'm going to call them and get them to send an ambulance.'

The hospital was Goodmayes, just a few miles from the house. But it might as well have been on Mars. 'No way, Nick. I'm not going.' We were shouting now and I think Nicola was scared I would totally lose it. I'm not sure how late it was. Maybe nine in the morning. Time meant nothing to me as I went on a long, loud rant. Colin Smith, who looked after things around the house, came in when he heard the noise. 'Come on, Frank. It's for the best.'

'No way. I'm not going anywhere.'

The ambulance arrived late in the morning or early in the afternoon. I couldn't be sure. There were doctors, nurses, all of them staring at me – just like people did when I got in the ring. Everybody telling me what to do. Do this, Frank. Do that, Frank. Just like they did when I worked on the building site as a teenager. Fetch this, Frank. Make the tea, Frank. I thought I'd left all that behind years ago, being ordered about.

It was a cool day but I was sweating like I was back on the

beach in Jamaica. Nicola and Colin tried to reason with me. But I wouldn't have it. I was out of control. It was so bad I couldn't understand what they wanted me to do. Words were tumbling out of my mouth but I wasn't sure what I was saying. And all I could hear coming back at me was some stuff from Nicola and what seemed like a thousand strangers.

Through all the noise, it hit me: whatever I wanted to do, they were going to take me away. It didn't matter what I thought. But it wasn't right, was it, that they could just come here to my house, throw me into an ambulance and drive me off to hospital?

I needed to be taken there. I might have been a danger to other people. I know that now. But I felt angry because I had no say in what was happening. They were in my house, uninvited. I have always valued my privacy – basically I'm a loner – and here were these total strangers standing in front of me in my kitchen telling me I had to go to hospital.

After a while, things turned ugly. I was surrounded by police. God knows where they came from. I'm not sure how, but they persuaded me to go outside. They jumped on top of me and I went down like an oak tree. They pulled me back to my feet. The world went fuzzy. I couldn't see straight, couldn't think straight. I could hear crying and shouting as they led me into the ambulance.

I'd never heard the term 'sectioned' before. I heard it now, just before the doors of the ambulance shut. A voice was telling me they were taking me away under Section 2 of the Mental Health Act. Apparently, I was a danger to myself and others.

I'd not been in a street fight since I was a kid in Wandsworth, but I wanted to lay them all out. I couldn't. My arms and legs weren't working for me any more. There were all these people telling me what to do. They kept saying, over and over, 'It's for your own good, Frank, it's for your own good . . .'

My mind's going numb, I can't understand what's happening. I'm up against the ropes with Tyson, and he's trying to tear my head off. I'm back in the ring at Wembley. Bonecrusher is bashing me to the floor. Or is it Jumbo Cummings? Or Tim Witherspoon? Or Lennox Lewis? Except I can't throw anything back.

Laura's here. Where did she come from? And there's my old mate Cass Pennant. It seems to have gone quiet. I look out the window of the ambulance and there are the photographers, like there were all my career. Snapping away. One flash after another. How did they know? They always did, though. They're never far away.

We're driving away from the house. I hear talking. Are they talking about me? Now we've stopped. This must be the hospital. They lead me out of the ambulance and through some doors. There are people inside, staring. Strangers, all of them, staring at me. Who are these people?

From somewhere, I find the strength to loosen up my arms. I try to shake some life into my legs. I'm swaying on my feet. I still can't make out what people are saying. I look in their eyes and all I see is confusion. And there's the door out of this terrible place. That's where I want to go.

'I want to go,' I tell them. Some guy tries to reason with me. Then it kicks off. I go for him and his friends get hold of me. We're struggling on the floor. I feel a needle jab into my backside. Like one of those poor bulls in a bullfight, I sink to my knees, and then I'm flat on my face. They have me down again. The noise is getting louder. They're pushing my face on to the cold, hard floor. My body goes limp. After a bit, I stop struggling. I want to fight them, but I can't. It's like being knocked out. Then I'm in another room and a doctor is talking to me. It's 3 a.m. and I'm exhausted.

When I came round, I was on my own again, in a small white room. The bed was barely big enough for me. There was a single pillow. The sheets were crisp and clean.

I didn't want to be in this place. I had to get out. But the door was closed. They had shut me into their world and it might as well have been a prison. I still had my one link to the outside, my mobile phone. I put it on the locker, next to the bedside lamp, which I didn't want to turn off. There was no clock. It might have been midnight. It might have been six in the morning. It could have been 1970, for all I knew.

A nurse put his head in to check on me. I looked up. 'You OK, Frank?' he said. 'You know you're in here for twenty-eight days. You might as well get used to it.' You must be mad, I thought to myself. It's funnier now than it was then.

'Goodnight, sir,' I said. He turned away and left. For several minutes, still dizzy, I just stared at the wall. I got undressed and lay down, looking up at the ceiling as my brain got heavier. I was confused and angry. My head felt like it was stuffed with cotton wool and my legs were like lead pipes. They'd knocked me off my feet but they hadn't totally calmed me down. I still had a bit of fight in me and they would get to see it in the days to come. I couldn't get over the fact they had taken me from my own house against my will. It was hard to keep hold of my thoughts because my mind was in a mess.

They had pumped me with drugs, the heavy ones with the long names. What else could they do? They were trying to control the former heavyweight champion of the world, a man who had knocked people unconscious for a living.

As I lay on the bed, my head throbbed and my eyelids started to close. 'What the hell am I doing here?' I thought. It's a question I'd asked myself all my life. Sometimes in the ring, I would look across at the guy in the other corner, the man I was being paid to hit, and think I was in a very strange business. But I wasn't forced to do it. I had chosen to make my living this way. At least in the ring I had some control. I had power in my fists. Now the drugs were stealing my brain. This was a different sort of fight. And I was afraid I couldn't win.

I was drifting off now, and my mind was finally calm. Sleep. This is what I wanted so badly, relief from all that had happened. Since I was a small boy, I had been cursed with too much energy. Some days I thought I'd explode. Sleep. It was the only way I could escape.

2

Twenty-Eight Days

MY FIRST NIGHT IN GOODMAYES WAS LIKE NOTHING I HAD EVER experienced. Not even like my first night at a boarding school in Sussex, when I missed my mum and thought I was going to end up a bad'un. Now I was an adult – and this was about my whole existence. I felt abandoned and alone. I'd faced some of the toughest heavyweights in the world, I'd been knocked out, I'd knocked them out too, I'd been a fighter all my life and survived in a sport that leaves strong men weak. And here I was, fighting for my sanity and my freedom.

What I've got, bipolar disorder, messes with your mind. There are two sides to it: when I'm really up my mind is racing for days and I can do some seriously weird things; at other times, I'm as low as it gets. All of this is why I was in Goodmayes.

I don't remember what time it was when I woke up in my small bedroom. I felt terrible. I hardly ever drink but I figured this must be what a hangover is like.

I got up, dressed and moved towards the door. I opened it slowly and looked out into the corridor. I was alone. I was in the men's section of Goodmayes' Pathways clinic. Ahead of me, a locked door separated us from the main part of the unit. A nurse let me through. It was like leaving the dressing room for a big fight.

This was going to be my first full day in a world of damaged people. I can't tell you how frightening that is, to come face to face with so much human sadness. And to be told that you are part of it, that you, too, are ill. I found myself staring at the other patients. There were fifteen of us, all sorts, men, women, black, white. It didn't matter where we were from, or who we were – we were all sharing the same secret. And there were twenty-seven days to go.

A long thin corridor led to the entrance, separated from us by two sets of locked doors. In our section, there were recreation rooms where you could sit and read, talk or watch television. One of them led out to a small patio and garden. There was even a room where you could smoke. In the kitchen a notice caught my eye. 'Fifteen knives, fifteen forks, fifteen spoons'. They had to be counted after every meal. Five nurses were on duty, doctors came and went. And on every door there were locks. What I felt was an awful sense of being cut off from the outside world, from my friends and family. I'd lost my freedom.

I normally don't have trouble eating, but I didn't feel much like breakfast that morning. On the menu was a bit of tea and toast – and my drugs.

After breakfast, I tried to chat to some of the other patients. 'Hello, ma'am, I'm Frank,' I said to one woman sitting by herself. She looked back at me and didn't say anything for a while. She told me her first name and said she'd been hooked on drugs and suffered a breakdown. It was hard to tell how ill she was. Hard to tell how ill I was, I suppose. I was still a bit wonky on my legs – and still angry.

I didn't think I belonged here. I don't mean to be disrespectful to those people still in that hospital or anyone else suffering from mental illness. I'm just telling it like it was for me at the time. What struck me was that there were all sorts of people in here. There was a middle-aged man who had been in business and lost everything, including his family. Another woman, very intelligent it seemed to me, said she was 'a bit of a regular'. She came in every so often, for a couple of months at a time. There were addicts, housewives, businessmen, 'duckers and divers', lost souls who just couldn't handle life. And there was a former heavyweight champion of the world. Most of the time you wouldn't know there was much wrong with them – or, should I say, with us.

They knew who I was but, for once, they weren't autograph hunters, they weren't journalists asking me questions, they weren't boxing promoters, they didn't want a piece of me. They weren't fans yelling my name. 'Broo-no! Broo-no!' They were patients in a mental hospital . . . just like me. They asked me why I was in here. I had no answer.

Pathways was a place where people normally weren't supposed to stay for very long. It was for emergency, short-term cases. People like me. Patients were here for six weeks on average. Six weeks can be a long time. I wondered if the others had anyone who had stuck by them. I knew I still had my family. They cared for me, even though they must have been shocked at how far I had fallen. There were a few old friends too.

Terry Lawless, my first manager, and Mickey Duff, my first promoter, were among the callers. They told me to keep battling away – like I had done my whole career. We'd had our differences – but that was business. I'd split with Terry in 1989, after my first fight with Mike Tyson. As for Mickey, I can't say we were close, but there were never really any hard feelings. They showed me they cared, and that counts for a lot.

As soon as she could, my sister Joan arrived. She told me about the *Sun*'s horrible headline: BONKERS BRUNO LOCKED UP. I didn't care, though. I was out of it. All I wanted was some peace of mind, my family and a quick taxi back to Stondon Massey.

'I'll come again tomorrow, Franklin,' Joan said. 'You take care now, and behave yourself.' She may be only a year older than me, but she's always kept an eye on her little brother, has Joan. She is as strong-minded as anyone I know.

My brother Michael and Nicola also turned up that day. They dragged me out of my despair but, too soon, they had to go. After they'd all gone, a sadness came over me again. I was back on my own.

I wandered through the recreation rooms. The television was on, probably one of those afternoon programmes like *Countdown*. There were magazines on the table. I didn't feel much like watching the TV and I've never been that keen on reading, except for my Bible. The place was clean and modern, only a couple of years old. It was a low-level security unit, but it was bright, comfortable and quiet. It couldn't have been more different from the only other mental hospital I'd seen.

In 1991, I'd gone with Jimmy Savile on one of his visits to

Broadmoor, the maximum-security psychiatric hospital for dangerous criminals. I was there to open a gym, and I met Peter Sutcliffe, the Yorkshire Ripper, and Ronnie Kray. Everywhere I looked in that horrible place were the empty eyes. A chill went down my back. I never wanted to end up in a place like that. I had to remind myself that Goodmayes was completely different.

There were no killers in Pathways. Just troubled people like me. But we were here through no choice of our own. And I got the feeling I was on trial. Each of us had our own battle to fight. We were here for many reasons: stress, drugs, drink, serious depression. Some of us were more fragile than others, although I came to realise that we were all vulnerable, no matter how tough we seemed to be on the outside. I tried hard not to let myself go. I was hanging on to my sanity.

I knew I had a choice to make: I could try to break out, or I could be smart. I had learnt discipline as a boxer. And I wasn't stupid. I knew who was in charge. I knew that as hard as I fought, I wouldn't be getting out. Not that I felt good about it. I was still fighting the world.

'Why?' I screamed at the doctors and nurses. 'Why am I in here? How can you do this to me? It's not right. You've got to let me out.'

The staff put up with no nonsense, and, looking back, I don't blame them. It's a tough job. They need to be firm. But I hated them at first. They told me it was for my own good. If I settled down and got better, they said, I'd be out soon.

I didn't believe them. Not straight away. I thought they were all lying, like a lot of people had lied to me in my life. I'd been in boxing long enough; I knew when someone was trying it on. Or so I thought. But I was so confused I didn't know what I was thinking. At the time, it felt like real *One Flew Over the Cuckoo's Nest* stuff, if you know that Jack Nicholson movie. How wrong can you get? Everyone was on my side. They didn't want me to be there any more than I wanted to be there.

The man in charge of helping me recover was Dr Stephen Pereira, one of the best psychiatrists in the country. He tried to explain to me how ill I was. I don't know if I took it in. He put me on a range of drugs to get me back on an even keel. Lithium I'd heard of; it stabilised my moods. I had to take a tranquilliser three or four times a day. And there was an anti-psychotic drug. They all had fancy names I couldn't pronounce. But I'd get to know them pretty well.

What I hadn't realised was how much total strangers cared, people who'd travelled thousands of miles to support me in my fights, or even those who had no interest at all in boxing. The phone calls, the flowers and letters of support started almost as soon as the papers had the story. It was touching, but confusing. It's a big responsibility to return so much affection, to know that people you've never met – and probably never will – can feel that warmly towards you.

Those first few days are still jumbled up in my head. But every night was the same. After my lithium, I was taken back to my room. I walked slowly, not feeling properly alive. I felt like I wasn't even a human being. I could eat and breathe for myself but everything else was decided for me.

I lay down on my bed and put my arms behind my head. Through the film working its way over my eyes I gazed at the patterns on the ceiling. Sometimes, patients would get upset and start crying before they went to sleep, one setting off another like a broken car alarm. It would die down soon enough but I knew it would start up again, a wave of frightening noise.

I tried to block everything out of my mind. I wondered if I would ever join this terrible choir.

The days that followed were more of the same. My body had to get used to the medication. I couldn't think straight much of the time and I felt heavy and useless. I'd been a fit athlete all my life and now I was walking around like an old man. An old, helpless man with no future, nowhere to go.

It took me a week at least to stop screaming at the staff. But I knew they cared. They asked you what you wanted to do – they didn't just order you about. They wanted you to get better, not spend the rest of your days locked up.

I soon found out there was a reason for the locked doors. It wasn't just security. They gave me order, a sense of self-discipline, when my mind was all over the place. I began to get some shape back into my life. In the morning I would get a dose of pills, play a little pool, chat to the others, lie down for a rest in the afternoon, have tea, some more pills . . . and then the part of the day I looked forward to. My room and sleep.

The other thing I looked forward to was visiting hour. My family, my friends – they were the ones who kept me going. One of the regulars was Dave Carroll, who used to drive for Frank Warren. 'Big Dave' we call him – a lovely bloke.

What struck me was how normal this weird world seemed to be once I got used to it. A lot of the time, we would talk about ordinary things, the weather, television programmes, what was in the papers. And then it would hit me: I didn't know what normal was any more.

In the months before I was admitted, I'd had the craziest sleeping patterns. I was exhausted and confused nearly every day. Now, I knew I was getting better: I started to drop off about nine o'clock each night, just as I used to as a fighter. It was like being back in training, almost as if I was making a comeback. When I fell asleep, I was winning the fight. It's all I wanted, to be left alone with my dreams. And every night, I knew I was that bit closer to freedom.

I'd stopped struggling against the system. There were a lot of good people in Pathways clinic – therapists, nurses, psychologists – and I must have made their lives hell to start with. Now I was cooperating with them. I couldn't have asked for better care. There were art and music classes, relaxation exercises. I did sessions to understand my illness, how it affected me and people around me. They wanted me to get involved, not just sit back and take my medicine. As I improved, they let me out for walks in the hospital grounds. Slowly, I felt better about life.

Dr Pereira explained to me a little bit about mental illness. It can hit anyone, and there is a lot of confusion about it. Nobody knows how many people it affects, but experts think at least one in twenty suffers from severe depression.

What I have is less common. There are different kinds of bipolar disorder – mine meant that sometimes I was restless, talked non-stop, couldn't concentrate and got seriously reckless. I'd become a danger to myself.

Dr Pereira said it was clear that this manic side, the 'up'

side, of my illness was more severe than the depressions. Before I was sectioned, I'd begun to lose touch with reality. I wasn't seeing things, I wasn't hallucinating, I wasn't what the doctors call 'delusional'. But I was paranoid and very suspicious of people.

I had to accept he was right, that I needed help. On the outside, I hadn't been able to help myself. Even so, I wanted to get home as soon as I could. After a couple of weeks, I was feeling a bit better, so I sat down with Dr Pereira, Laura and Joan to talk about my progress.

What worried me was they might never let me out. People who commit murder don't get put away for the rest of their days. What crime had I committed, except being a human being who'd cracked under pressure?

I thought I'd been doing OK, but Dr Pereira reminded me it wasn't over yet. If I wanted to see out my time in Pathways clinic – if I really wanted to get better – I had to calm down, engage with the staff and the treatments. If I didn't get better, they'd have no choice but to keep me in. That wouldn't be at Goodmayes, though. There were other centres, medium-level units, where patients stayed a lot longer. And there were maximum-security units – which I didn't even want to think about. I remembered Broadmoor and Ronnie Kray. He was there until the day he died.

So I listened. Thank God I listened. I'd do whatever they wanted. I'd play the piano. I'd paint. I'd talk to them all day long about my illness.

'You can stay here, Frank,' Dr Pereira said. 'I want you to get well – and I want you to help us to do that.' I was as relieved as a condemned man getting a last-minute pardon.

For the first time in years, I was focused again. When I was a boxer, my goal was always my next fight. It was my purpose for living, to get to the top, to be champion of the world. That's what kept me going through the toughest times. The doctors had given me another challenge. Just a few more weeks of behaving myself, showing them I was getting better, and I'd be free.

By this stage I was a lot calmer. I wouldn't say I was on top of the world, but I had come through the worst part of the storm. I was eating well, they had cut the drugs dosage levels. I was sleeping better every night. That was a big relief. Gradually, I was coming back to normal.

In the end I stayed on past my twenty-eight days. The extra weeks helped a lot. The nightmare was passing, and the staff knew I was well enough to be trusted. A couple of times towards the end, they even let me leave the hospital for a few hours to get used to the world again.

Outside, the photographers from the papers turned up every day, waiting for a glimpse of 'Bonkers Bruno'. I know they were only doing their job, but I think it's a funny way to make a living. At least while they were wasting their time on me, they weren't bothering anyone else.

Then it came, the moment I had been dreaming about ever since I'd cracked under the strain of just being Frank Bruno. On 21 November I heard the sweetest words I'd heard in weeks. 'Come on, Frank. You can go now. Your daughter's here.'

The day I was released was as good as winning the heavyweight championship of the world. Nicola, as ever, was there for me. We didn't say much. When you think about it, spending eight weeks in a mental hospital is not a great conversation starter. For the last time, I went to my bedroom. I took a quick look around, packed my bags and headed back to the reception desk to sign my release papers. I said goodbye to the staff – two in particular, Sam and John, had been a great help to me – and a few of the patients. I'd got close to a couple of them; we'd chatted about life, opened up a little to each other about our problems. I can't tell you their names because I have to respect their privacy. They said they'd ring me – when they could top up their mobiles. And they did. Much later, I went back to see them.

Slowly and nervously, I walked back into the outside world alongside Nicola. We somehow managed to dodge most of the photographers, got into her car and headed for Stondon Massey.

As she drove, she asked the inevitable question: 'How are you, Dad?' Not an easy one to answer, that. I was a little confused and I felt like I'd swallowed a chemist's shop. At least I was a free man. Instead of the screaming of patients, I heard the hum of the road and the wind rushing through the trees.

'Much better,' I said. And I had improved. But I'd just been through the most horrific experience of my life – and every day I live in fear of ever going back.

Nicola may have been driving me home, but it wasn't the home we had all loved. It was just a house now. A big, empty house full of memories, most of them brilliant, some of them sad. What would life be like now? I thought. Where would I go from here? I knew I had the support of my family, but I would have to do this myself. It was my responsibility. I had been given the biggest shock you can imagine, worse than any punch, and I had somehow come out the other side. If I didn't want to go through that terror again, it was up to me. Nobody else.

We pulled into the driveway and the sun was shining weakly on the front door. Inside were all the trinkets and gadgets, the big television, the phones and the trophies and the stuff you collect. Outside there were seventy-five acres, the cars, the tractors, the machines I'd bought and not even known how to use. There was the boxing ring, haunting me.

I had nobody to share this useless junk with.

Nicola gave me one more hug. I felt like crying but didn't. I didn't want to upset her. 'Take care, Dad,' she said. 'I'll call you tomorrow.' She turned and left. I closed the door. I'd never felt so lonely.

I looked at the pictures of my two daughters and my young son. I looked at the pictures of Laura. If I needed courage to get in the ring with Tyson and all the other headbangers I'd met in my career, I needed a different sort of courage now.

All I had were a hundred regrets and a thousand doubts . . . Then I looked in a corner and saw several big boxes. I opened one up and inside were cards and letters from the people who used to cheer my name. I opened another box, and another. There must have been 10,000 cards and letters in there. For a moment, I could hear the echoes of the crowd again. 'Broo-no! Broo-no!'

I looked out over the ropes into the dark, out past the harsh TV lights, and saw the thousands of smiling faces. People waved and shouted as if they had known me all their lives.

We were standing in the ring at Wembley Stadium. I turned and saw George Francis in my corner. 'Well done, Frank. You've done it at last, son. Heavyweight champion of the world.' I looked down and saw Nigel Benn, grinning like he always did. In the other corner was the man I'd just beaten to win the title, Oliver McCall. Oliver didn't look so clever. But this was my night. They said I couldn't do it, and I proved them wrong. I proved them all wrong . . .

3

Country Days

PROBABLY NOT MANY KIDS HAVE RUN OVER WESTMINSTER BRIDGE faster than I did that day in 1972. I had good reason to hurry. I had just wrestled my teacher to the ground while we were on a school trip to the Houses of Parliament. I got the impression he wasn't too happy about it.

I wasn't a mean kid. I just had so much energy to get rid of. It was a mystery to me where it came from. The fire inside me has always been there. That day, though, I got into one scrap too many.

I'd been fooling about with one of the girls in the class, trying to take her camera away from her, when the teacher stepped in. The camera fell to the ground and so did he and so did I. It was no more than a tussle, believe me. Years later someone wrote that I knocked him out cold, which is nonsense – I was only eleven. It lasted maybe ten seconds. If I landed a punch on him it was accidental. It was just a bit of pushing and shoving. And there may have been a cross word or two.

What I did realise was that he would use this against me. He would tell the headmaster I'd been trying to hit him – and there wasn't much doubt about whose story the headmaster would believe. I wasn't in the habit of beating up my teachers, though. This man and I just didn't get on. He thought I was a bully and I reckoned he was a bit flash. But I knew my limits. There was a line you didn't cross.

I admit I could be a bit lippy. Where I grew up in south London, that's the way it was, and still is. It was how we talked to each other. There wasn't much 'yes sir, no sir'. If you could get away with a smart remark, you would. You'd always be taking the mickey out of your friends and, sometimes, adults. I meant no serious disrespect by it.

I'd have the odd fight as well, inside and outside school. Fighting was also part of growing up in south London. I never considered myself a bully, but my father wasn't convinced. Especially when other kids' parents kept coming round to complain about me. Dad spent the last five years of his life in bed, a big, strong man wasting away with diabetes, heart problems and a stroke that paralysed him down one side. 'Franklin, come over here,' he would say after I had been called up to his bed. 'You know it's time for the curtain rod.' But no amount of canings could stop me getting into trouble. I was like a battery that wouldn't run down.

My other problem was what turned out to be my biggest asset: my size. Anyone who has outgrown his mates knows how easy it is to become a target. And I was never one to turn down a challenge. The trouble is I liked it. Not because I wanted to hurt anyone, but because it was the one sure way I knew of coping with all this energy that built up inside me.

This time, though, I had gone too far. When I ran home to Barmouth Road I knew I was in for it. Soon enough my mother found out what had happened. I begged her not to take me in to school the next day. She was having none of it. 'Franklin,' she said, 'tomorrow you're going to be in big trouble.'

'You just don't listen, Frank,' the headmaster said as I stood before him. 'I can't remember how many warnings I've given you for fighting at school. Now you've hit a teacher. I can't let that go unpunished. You're expelled.'

Mum said nothing. I didn't take it in at first. I wondered what exactly an eleven-year-old boy did if he didn't go to school. I was about to find out.

'I'm sending you to a special school, Frank. It's a place for boys who have had a problem with discipline. I hope you make the most of this opportunity – it could be the last one you get.'

I looked up at my mother, Lynette. There might have been a tear in her eye, I can't remember. There might have been one in my eye for that matter. Some bully I was. She didn't speak to me on the way home. I knew I was in for an even tougher time from my father.

My mother comes from Jamaica. She's a cheerful but strictly religious woman, who worked as a district nurse. She had four kids already when I arrived – all nine pounds of me – at Hammersmith Hospital in 1961. From my earliest days, I was a handful. I would throw toys around, try to break the rails on my cot, shout my head off in the house my parents had found for us in Wandsworth. The day I started school at Swaffield Primary, I ran home – and was dragged back by my mother. My sisters – Faye, Angela and Joan – as well as my brother Michael must have had a good laugh.

Despite what some people have said, our part of Wandsworth was no ghetto. Barmouth Road today, as it was then, is a quiet road full of big Victorian houses. I reckon some of them must be worth close to £1 million these days. I was joking with my mother a while ago that maybe we should have stayed there a bit longer. We were among the first black families in the area, but I don't remember that being a problem. Anyway, as a child, you're often protected from that sort of thing.

My mother was a Pentecostal preacher, so we were always reminded of what would happen to us if we didn't behave. She may have been strict, but I was more scared of my father, Robert. More scared of him, too, than I was of anyone at school – or anyone in the world, come to that – and I knew it was no laughing matter to be expelled. He was a classic West Indian dad, very loving but always firm. Nobody deserves the bad luck that came his way.

My father left Dominica in the fifties, but he never found the life he was looking for here. He got a job as a warehouseman in a bakery and, before he could establish himself, his health started to go. More and more, he was off work. Eventually, he ended up bedridden. I know it was a big blow to his pride.

All his life my father supported the West Indies cricket team. He made no apologies about it – why should he have? I used to sit with him sometimes, listening to Test matches on the radio, and my early heroes were all West Indian, Gary Sobers particularly. Sobers, the greatest cricketer of them all, was a god to everyone from the Caribbean. But I've always supported England. After all, it's where I was born. And I'm very proud to be British.

My other hero was Muhammad Ali and, as I got bigger, I think my father knew I was more likely to be a fighter than a cricketer. That's why he bought me my first pair of boxing gloves.

I was eight when he took me down to join the Wandsworth Boys' Club. Mum thought it was a good idea, too. 'You'll burn off some of that energy, Franklin,' she said (my parents always used my full name). 'And maybe you'll stop getting into fights with other kids.'

I knew from the first punch I threw that this was the game for me, although my debut wasn't a roaring success. The only boy my size they could find was Gary Levington. He was the son of the trainer and five years older than me. As mismatches go, it wasn't a bad one. Gary, who went on to become a policeman and a good friend, was already an experienced junior amateur. He was a southpaw, too, which meant he led with his right hand rather than his left, as most fighters do. He was so awkward I could hardly lay a glove on him. Welcome to boxing, I thought.

I was back the following night, though, and for as many nights as I could cram in after that. I was never brilliant at school, so boxing became the centre of my life. It burnt up some of the energy that was getting me into trouble. In my first year I even won a national title. I did it the easy way. I got a bye in every round, including the final. The National Association of Boys' Clubs just couldn't find anyone big enough to fight me. So I was a champion without having to throw a single punch.

Even so, my serious fighting days were a little way off. My parents were happy enough just knowing where I was after school. But they weren't the only ones looking out for me. If there was a row, my sister Joan would be in the middle of it. 'Franklin,' she'd say, 'I'm the one who should have been the fighter.' I would be around the corner, laughing.

My hero was my brother Michael. He is twelve years older than me, a very big man, but I never asked him to fight my battles. If I got into a row, I would settle it myself, sometimes a bit too roughly. I probably terrorised a few of the local kids, but I wouldn't listen when people told me what to do. From my earliest days I was stubborn. Later, I would learn to swim with the tide.

We were a very happy family, and I couldn't have asked for better. Mum cooked all the Caribbean meals you've heard about, the chicken and fish and rice and peas, good wholesome food. On the street, I could still be a handful. But at home, we all did as we were told. Every Sunday we'd go along to my mother's church in Fulham, and I loved the singing and the atmosphere. There's nothing like it, a hall full of people feeling good and singing those beautiful gospel songs.

I was learning to box and trying to stay out of trouble. Then, for the only time in my life, I got drunk. I was just eight years old. A friend and I found a barrel of beer sitting there in the street in Wandsworth, believe it or not. We weren't sure what it was at first. So we got it open and necked it. The lot. I don't know how much we drank, maybe a few pints. But we were off our heads. Then I went home and disgraced myself. I was sick all over the place and swearing at everyone.

'Franklin, what's the matter with you?' my mother said. I won't say what I said back to her but it wasn't very nice.

Mum, as a nurse, understood what was happening. In the end she was laughing her head off. It was a scary experience, but I suppose it did me a favour. It put me off alcohol for ever, apart from the odd glass of wine with a meal now and again. Growing up in south London, I would see my mates getting drunk every Friday and Saturday night. But it wasn't for me. I would discover a different drug.

I wasn't Mike Tyson, but I was running wild, chilling on the corner with my mates, doing a bit of shoplifting, picking fights. I saw no great harm in it because nothing awful ever happened. A few of my friends ended up in prison. I might have done as well if it weren't for my parents. My mother used to pray for me. Dad preferred more earthly solutions. And every time I got into trouble I broke their hearts.

The rumble with my teacher was pretty serious. 'Franklin,' my father said, 'you're to go to this school and change your ways. If you don't, you know you might go down the wrong path. And you know you'll have me to answer to.'

Usually when I went into the bedroom to see my father, it was to give him his injection of insulin. This time, it was to say sorry and goodbye. I left to pack my bags. I was going to be away for five years and I was homesick before I left the house. I'd hardly ever been out of Wandsworth, let alone London. Now I was off to Oak Hall, a big old house in the middle of nowhere.

'Make the most of it, Franklin,' my mother said. 'It might be the best thing that ever happened to you.'

I was on my own for the first time in my life. As we got closer to Oak Hall, twisting our way down tiny old lanes somewhere in Sussex, I couldn't have felt further away from the noisy streets of south London. I didn't like it one bit. Oak Hall was a boarding school, but not exactly like Harry Potter's. At any one time, it was home to sixty or so of the roughest diamonds in London. Now I was one of them.

They'd told us Oak Hall was in the country so I knew we were getting close when we passed a few grand old houses, surrounded by fields. The last one I saw was at the top of the lane running down to the school. It was an old people's home run by a nice man called Mr Chapman. Later I would go to work for him. One day I would own a house even bigger than his.

Oak Hall had a fascinating past. It was an Edwardian manor house left to the old Greater London Authority by Sir Harry Oakes. Oakes was one of the richest men in the world and quite an item. During the Second World War he lived in the Bahamas and mixed with some interesting characters, apparently. The Duke of Windsor and his American wife, Wallis Simpson, were good friends. There were also Nazi sympathisers, spies, gamblers, playboys and assorted gangsters. In 1943 Oakes was found burnt and battered to death in his bed.

I cried myself to sleep that first night. And many nights after that. I really didn't want to be in this house. I really didn't want to be stuck in here with all these wild kids. All my life people have been telling me what's good for me – teachers, trainers, managers, promoters, lawyers. And then along came the doctors with their syringes.

Back then I blamed my mother for letting me be banged up. I know now it was for my own good. But I didn't think that when I ran into Gunter Roomes. It hadn't taken me long to work out there were some seriously hard customers at Oak Hall, and one of the hardest was Gunter. 'Oi, Bruno,' he said, 'if you know what's good for you in here, you'll do as I tell you. If you do, you'll be all right. If not . . . well, that's up to you.'

Gunter was a black kid from Eltham, a no-nonsense part of south-east London. But he wasn't as bad as he sounded. In fact he was OK, Gunter. I figured he was just trying it on with the new boy. Actually he never touched me. Maybe it was because, even though he was three years older, we were the same size. And we found we had something else in common. 'So, you're a bit of a boxer, Bruno,' he said. I wasn't too keen on developing this conversation. I reckoned Gunter was just looking for an excuse to belt me one. 'Yeah, Gunter, I'm a boxer . . . but not in here.'

I soon found out they didn't allow competitive boxing at Oak Hall. It was a real blow. The one thing I called my own they wouldn't let me have. It was my way of expressing myself. The boxing ring was where I felt comfortable and safe. Since I'd discovered boxing, I had started to calm down a little – whatever my teachers thought.

But the GLA reckoned it was unsafe – even for young boys who couldn't knock the top off a custard. I thought it was wrong then, because it was my sport. I think it's wrong now because I know how much good it can do for overactive boys. Whatever they called it, Oak Hall was a reform school. We were not exactly choirboys. We weren't scared of a little rough and tumble, so boxing would have been brilliant for us. It teaches respect, builds character and it helps young kids let off steam. Believe me, there was plenty of steam at Oak Hall.

As the weeks went by, I tried to keep my head down. I wasn't looking for trouble, and I even became friends with Gunter. But I was still homesick. I thought about running away. One of the teachers got wind of it and said, 'Why don't you give it another go, Frank? If you run away now, you'll only make things worse for yourself.' She was right. So I stayed. And I'm glad I did.

Oak Hall was a schoolboy's heaven. We may not have been Mensa candidates but, outside the classroom, we couldn't have asked for a better education. There was cricket, football, canoeing, horse riding, judo, tennis, cross-country running and basketball. I tried them all.

I played a decent standard of football, good enough to be picked for Sussex Schools. I was a striker and I always imagined I was Peter Osgood. Still, I was never going to play for Chelsea – there wasn't quite enough twinkle in my toes.

In the summer I made the school cricket team. I bowled fast and, when everything clicked, pretty straight. My cricket heroes have always been the great West Indian fast bowlers. Again, the comparison was a bit ambitious. I was probably more Devon Malcolm than Malcolm Marshall. With all due respect to Devon.

When we weren't on the pitch, we had outings to the seaside, to Eastbourne and Hastings. We went camping, where I learnt to cook. There was plenty of fresh air and exercise, a real contrast with Wandsworth. I even learnt to play the piano, although I never threatened to be a concert pianist – my fingers were too big for the keys.

I slowly came to appreciate the efforts of the teachers, even if some were more understanding than others. I got on well with Mr Lawrence, the headmaster, and Mr Irwin, the sports master, who was a big boxing fan. The discipline was strict – there were forfeits and penalties if you misbehaved, and I felt the weight of the slipper too many times for my liking – but they encouraged you to think for yourself.

Despite their best efforts, there was still a lot of Wandsworth in me. Every holiday I was back in Barmouth Road, and I would look up my old mates. I was about twelve or thirteen and on a summer break when I had my first joint. I'm not going to say who gave it to me as I don't know that he'd appreciate it. But let's just say it wasn't too hard to come by where I grew up. I didn't enjoy it at first. It made me paranoid. I was always looking round the corner to see if we were going to get caught. But I grew to like my bit of puff – not that I was smoking every day. It was just a way to chill out occasionally. I'm a black Briton from south London; marijuana is part of my culture. People shouldn't have a problem with that.

I returned to Oak Hall with a spring in my step, feeling a bit more grown up. But I was barely in my teens and I had some rough times ahead. My father's health was getting worse by the month, and one afternoon during a football match I snapped. The referee had really wound me up with a dumb decision and I lost it. I started ranting and raving at him. It was the sort of behaviour that had landed me here in the first place. He sent me to see the deputy head – and that's when it kicked off.

One minute we were standing in the library then, before I knew it, we were rolling around all over the place, tables, chairs and books going in all directions. I don't think too many serious blows were landed but it was a bit of a perform-ance. It took the house parent to get us apart. I thought for sure I would be kicked out, but somehow I survived.

That was a turning point, probably the last time I lashed out at authority as a teenager. I realised there were more important things in life, like the failing health of my father. I used to think about him every day and it put a few things in perspective.

When I was about fourteen, I became a Catholic. It was my father's religion and, although he was lapsed, I thought it might comfort him. My mother probably would have preferred me to be a member of her congregation, but that's the way it went. To this day, religion plays a part in my life, although not in a loud or obvious way. There have been times in my life when a quiet prayer has got me through a tough patch. My trainer, George Francis, was also a Catholic, and we often spoke about how our religion helped us. In the end, though, you have to handle things yourself. I never could work out why fighters like Evander Holyfield would try to bring God into their corner. I'm pretty sure He doesn't have favourites.

What I really craved was not religion but boxing. While the GLA wouldn't let us box competitively, Oak Hall did have a ring and we were allowed to spar. I'd learnt the basics at

Wandsworth Boys' Club and Mr Irwin could see my potential. He was happy to take me to the gym and show me what he knew.

I was growing up fast, in every way. And boxing was a big part of it. It was just me and the other guy. I didn't have to rely on anyone else. If I did well, it was down to me; if I didn't, that was my lookout too. It's a peculiar buzz. There is nothing like it. The ring is the loneliest place in sport – and the most exciting. You bring all your history with you. If you have misbehaved, if you haven't trained properly, if you're underdone, boxing will find you out. Nobody is safe from the examination. I think that's why I was attracted to it. If you threw that right hand and it landed properly, you got the result you deserved. If you'd skimped on your training and you weren't up for it, you could bet the other guy would be in there finding you out. It was the best education I ever had.

There is only one way to learn how to box: do it. At Oak Hall all I had was my occasional sparring. And sometimes they would tell us to settle our arguments with the gloves on. But it was so frustrating. From the first proper blows I landed, I knew I had the one thing you can't buy or make: power. I had these huge hands and a body that was growing faster than any of my friends.

I struggled through my maths, history, geography and English, all the time gazing out the window, wondering about my future. I knew I didn't want to spend the rest of my life on a building site. In some parts of London, thieving and fighting have always been the easiest alternatives. I could still feel the sting of the curtain rod my father kept beside his bed – I didn't want to lead that sort of life, either. Even then, it was obvious how I was going to make my living.

Every day, tens of thousands of boys dream about making it big in sport. In the end, nearly all of them find it too tough. The training and sacrifices you have to make, in any sport, are enormous. In boxing they can break the hardest kid. But I was more determined than most. I'd seen how I might end up if I failed to make it. I knew I could whack; what I didn't know yet was, could I box?

I would talk about this with my brother Michael whenever I was back in Barmouth Road. I told him how I used to dream about Muhammad Ali, dream that I was him, that I was a champion. Michael had already written just that on our kitchen wall: FRANK BRUNO, HEAVYWEIGHT CHAMPION OF THE WORLD, 1986. He didn't get the year right, but I would prove him right in the end.

Those trips home were not always happy ones. When my mother was on her rounds or my sisters were out of the house, I would hear the call that I dreaded from my father upstairs. I would go and get the syringe and the insulin. I hated seeing him in such pain. Then, after I had pushed the needle into him, there would be relief on his face and he'd smile. 'Thanks, Franklin,' he'd say. 'You're a good boy, really.'

The weeks grew into months and the months into years at Oak Hall. I left behind me a lot of the bad habits of my youth. In my last term they made me one of the head boys, which was an honour, as well as an opportunity to prove myself. Mr Lawrence and his staff even let me go to a village dance in nearby Broadoak on my own. I also got to know Mr Chapman in the big house at the top of the lane. I worked part-time for him, cleaning the cars, clearing up the chicken shit, polishing the floor, pretty much anything that needed doing. I felt I was growing into a young man who could be trusted.

I was going to miss my ragamuffin classmates. No more cigarettes behind the shed (it was going to be herbs of a slightly stronger nature). No more riding horses or canoeing. No more schoolyard brawls. But I would miss the staff too. Oak Hall had become our second home, a special place run by people who cared about us. They wanted you to be the best person you could be. I might not have been the most brilliant student with books, but I learnt from my many mistakes. I came to see the good in people. Those were my days of innocence and I treasure them. When I left Oak Hall, I knew I'd never get them back.

4

Almost a Man

BY THE TIME I GOT BACK TO WANDSWORTH MY FATHER HAD DIED. Even before I arrived, I somehow knew he'd gone. I was fifteen and in my last few months at Oak Hall, having a sly cigarette behind the shed with some of the boys. And then I heard my father's voice. I swear that's what happened, and it really shook me up. It meant something was wrong. Maybe he was calling out to me because he knew he couldn't hang on until I got there. It was the saddest day of my young life.

Soon after, I was home for good. It was wicked to be back. Although I'd lost my father, or maybe *because* I had, I was determined to put my wild days behind me. For a lot of teenage boys, especially where I grew up, losing your dad can lead to all sorts of trouble. I'd learnt my lesson at Oak Hall.

My mother noticed the change in me. I'd calmed down, and I wanted to make something of my life. I had grown up in more ways than one. Some of my friends were already getting into serious trouble and I was having none of it.

Sometimes it's hard not to be distracted by your friends. I've got some mischief in me but I usually try to do the right thing. I had to find a way to use what talents I had.

I joined the Sir Philip Game Amateur Boxing Club in Croydon, again benefiting from the generosity of a dead toff. Air Vice-Marshal Sir Philip, to give him his full title, had been the Commissioner of the Metropolitan Police. Along the way, he established the club that was to be my boxing home for the next few years, the place where, under the guidance of Freddy Rix, I would learn my craft as I grew into a heavyweight.

In my early days I struggled to find novice boxers my size – I was a good fifteen stone and over six feet tall – so I had to fight men much older than me. I didn't lack for confidence, just experience. Already people were talking about me because of my big punch. I was getting used to the training regime under Freddy, and I made it down to Croydon as often as I could.

I won my first two fights without much fuss. But I had a setback in my third fight. I came up against a seasoned Irishman called Joe Christle, who beat the absolute granny out of me for three rounds. I was lucky to make it to the bell. He was Irish tough, and hard to box because he had all the moves. What a fight. But not my favourite night of boxing, I can tell you. Joe was an international and I was a young amateur, still learning the game. I learnt more about looking after myself that night than in a lot of my fights as a pro.

I didn't have many problems after the Christle fight, and Freddy was happy with my progress. A lot of opponents were intimidated by my size and physique – and my left hook. I was slowly putting together basic combinations: left jab, left hook, right cross, uppercut. I wasn't concentrating too much on defence at the time because not many of the bouts lasted that long. They tend to stop fights early in the amateurs.

I would be eighteen soon, old enough for the national championships. It looked like my dream was coming true. But would I be able to cut it in the pros? There was one good way to find out.

Amateurs and pros weren't supposed to train together, but everyone did it. I wanted to see for myself what it was like in a professional gym and George Francis seemed like the perfect man to go to. George was one of the best in the business – he was training John Conteh at the time – and one day in 1978 I wandered into his Highgate gym, at the back of the Wellington pub, looking for some quality sparring. I liked George from the moment we met. Although, from his attitude, I wasn't sure what he reckoned of me. I was a big, raw seventeen-year-old who had shown up unannounced. He'd seen me at a few amateur shows but his business was preparing the paid boys.

'I'd like to spar, please, sir,' I said to him.

'Would you now?' he said. 'In you get then.'

I stripped down and got in the ring, went three rounds – I can't remember who with – and thought that was it. George soon put me right. 'You finish when I say,' he said, pointing me back into the ring for another three rounds.

I was young, fit and strong, though, and I think I handled it pretty well. George got me on the floor exercises, put me on the big bag to look at my power, then the speedball to see how my reflexes were. I finished off with a bit of skipping. I'm sure he thought a big ungainly lump like me would fall over his own feet but I did OK.

George was an extremely generous man, in every way, but you couldn't take liberties with him. That first day I wanted some money for my efforts and he looked at me as if I'd asked him for the keys to his house. He did give me a fiver for my fare back to south London. He made it clear it was 'just this time', then he asked me to come back again. He even suggested I move into a house in Hampstead with one of his other fighters so I could be closer to the gym. I knew he must have been impressed with me.

This is it, I thought. Proper training with a man who works with world champions. And I would be working out in the same gym as John Conteh, who was a hero of mine, a genuine character and a great boxer. John had a real strut about him. He was a dashing Scouser with a good line in jokes and chat-up for the girls. He didn't waste his talents in that regard, that's for sure.

Though I was still boxing for the Sir Philip Game, I settled in quickly at the Wellington. I had been brought up to show respect to my elders and it was natural for me to call George 'sir'. But that wasn't his way. So, from the beginning, George it was. That summer, I got a real feeling for how it was to prepare as a professional. It gave me a lot of confidence. If I could handle myself in a pro gym already, I reckoned I wouldn't disgrace myself when the time came to leave the amateurs behind. What could possibly stop me now?

After my sessions with George, I felt more confident about

my next big challenge: a rematch with Joe Christle. What I learnt most from that fight was how your past experiences can affect you. I could remember every punch he hit me with two years before and I didn't want to go through that again. But, if I was going to make it in boxing, I would have to overcome those doubts. It was going to be tough, especially as the bout was away from home, at the Stardust Club in Dublin.

I'll be blunt: I was shitting myself. It wasn't the physical pain I was worried about. It never is in boxing, because your adrenalin is rushing through you so fast you don't notice the bruises. It was the mental pressure. I didn't want to be embarrassed like I had been the first time. That's what matters most to a fighter, your dignity. I knew how good Joe was and we were in his home town. I didn't want to go out there in front of a hostile crowd and make a fool of myself.

I won that night. It was the night I knew for sure I could make it as a fighter. I had overcome my doubts and put in a pretty good performance against a seasoned heavyweight. I wasn't the only one who thought I'd fought well. The papers were starting to take notice. Everyone wants a heavyweight prospect. The Dubliners, who love their amateur boxing, turned out in force – they gave me a wonderful reception. I just hope there weren't any of them there when the club burnt down shortly afterwards.

I knew I wasn't going to stay in the amateurs much longer. The professional managers and promoters had been sniffing about for some time and I was listening. As a metal polisher, I was bringing home £43 a week. It was the dirtiest job of my life. Then I was a plumber's humper, which is exactly what it sounds like. I humped all manner of things – toilets, baths, taps, pipes – up and down stairs for the boss. After that, I embarked on my third 'career', a gofer on a building site. They were all dead-end jobs and they left me knackered at the end of the day. On top of that, I had to train.

I don't regret those days, as they taught me a lot about hard graft. They also made me appreciate the big money I would later earn. My father had instilled in all of us the virtues of hard work, but I also wanted some hard currency for it. And I wasn't going anywhere on the building site. Especially not in my old banger.

Every day, professional boxing looked more attractive. A lot of people were telling me I should stay amateur, go for medals, the Olympics and all that. They were saying I should be proud to represent my country – and I always was. But generally they didn't have to worry about where their next pay packet was coming from. Boxing was my love and my life. It was also my only way to earn proper money. The journalists writing the stories about me had far more opportunities in life than I'd ever had.

Besides, the amateur game is riddled with politics. The Amateur Boxing Association is run by men with very fixed views. You can miss out on the big international tournaments just because the national coach doesn't like your style or has had a row with your club coach. Even though I was improving quickly, I didn't think I was a good bet to qualify for the Olympics, and I didn't see much point carrying on if I was only going to be boxing the same guys again in Britain.

In the end, I won twenty out of twenty-one of my amateur fights. That last season, in 1980, I finished on a real high.

It was my first time in the ABA championships and in my last fight I beat the Welshman Rudi Pika to win the heavyweight title. I had a broken bone in my left hand, although I never told anyone at the time, and Rudi gave me a very hard fight. I was the youngest heavyweight champion the amateur game ever had, and the men with the chequebooks could hardly wait to start making money with me. I discussed it with my brother Michael and made my mind up. I had one chance and I went for it. All those dreams I'd had at Oak Hall about becoming the heavyweight champion of the world were about to be put to the test. I could hardly wait.

As I grew towards adulthood, I became aware of the gift I had: the ability to knock another human being unconscious with a single blow. It might sound terrible when you say it like that, but I looked on the power God gave me as my only way to be the best person I could be. This is not merely justifying my trade. It's what I believe. If I had ever doubted it, I wouldn't have been able to box for a living. I was never troubled by using that power, letting it go with as much force as I could and bringing my night's work to the quickest possible end. Expecting me to hold back would be like asking an airline pilot to drive you along the road in his jumbo jet.

The papers were talking me up more and more as a real prospect. This country hadn't had a world heavyweight champion since Bob Fitzsimmons knocked out James J. Corbett in 1897. Like Mike Tyson, I might not have spent much time with my schoolbooks but I knew my boxing history. And I'd heard a lot about Fitzsimmons. When I won the undisputed title myself, it was an honour to be linked through a direct line of fighters all the way back to him. He left Cornwall as a small boy, and grew up in New Zealand and Australia, where he fought bareknuckled, sometimes four or five times on the same night. When he moved to the United States as a young man, he used his wife as a sparring partner. Which is not something you'd want people to know.

Fitzsimmons kept boxing until he was fifty-one and he claimed he had 350 fights. I was determined my career would be shorter and more lucrative. As much as I loved it, as much as I wanted to be world champion, boxing was also a job. I had to make sure it brought me a good return. People often forget when they see the big money champions can earn that our working lives are short. For nearly all boxers, the real pay days never arrive, and that must be heartbreaking for those guys who start out with great ambitions. It's one reason you'll never hear boxers laughing behind Chris Eubank's back, as weird as people think he is. Chris knew how to work the system.

Now I needed someone to look after my career. The noise I made as an amateur had alerted the professionals. The word was out among other fighters because I was impressing George Francis in sparring at his gym. Freddy Rix introduced me to Frank Maloney, who would later get lucky with Lennox Lewis. Terry Lawless, one of the best managers in the country, saw me win the ABA title. He mentioned me to a business associate of his, Mickey Duff, the promoter. It was all happening for me.

I decided Terry was the man for me. I didn't get the impression he was trying to schmooze me, like some of the others. He'd started out as a tally clerk in the docks and could handle himself. Although he'd never boxed in his life, he knew the game as well as anyone I've ever met. Obviously I'd heard about him, and about his world champions: Jim Watt, John H. Stracey and Maurice Hope. He'd never worked with a heavyweight but, then again, there weren't many he reckoned were worth working with.

I didn't stay with George because I was joining Terry's team at the Royal Oak gym in Canning Town. Terry had his own trainers and his own methods. He was an old-fashioned boxing man who ran things his way. He didn't like music in the gym, for instance. He'd never left the East End and he surrounded himself with people he knew and trusted. I was sorry to leave George behind but it was the right thing to do at the time. The Royal Oak was full of champions. There was a buzz about the place and I knew I was going to get serious attention there.

Terry's role as a manager was straightforward. He would decide who, when and where I fought. He provided the gym and the trainers and, in the end, he was responsible for my development as a boxer. From day one he made it clear he was spending a lot of money on me. He regarded it as an investment. Terry's share of my earnings wouldn't be that big to start with, he said. When the purses got bigger, then we'd all be earning a fair whack. Especially if I became the heavyweight champion of the world.

Terry had known Mickey, Jarvis Astaire and Mike Barrett for years. Mickey was the promoter, which meant he arranged the overall deal. It was his job to set up the hall, the dates, sell the tickets and the TV rights. Jarvis and Mike were responsible for the venues. Jarvis had been in show business and boxing most of his life, and he had access to Wembley.

Mike, another old pro, had access to the Royal Albert Hall. This meant that I'd be fighting at the two major boxing venues in the country.

I knew professional boxing was a jungle. I needed someone I could depend on. From the moment we met, I liked Terry. I said once, and I meant it, that I would trust him with my life. I liked his wife Sylvia, too, and got to know his whole family as if they were my own. Before big fights, I often stayed at Terry's home in Emerson Park, Essex, hanging out with his son Stephen and his daughter Lorraine, stuffing myself on Sylvia's home cooking. Terry himself was an unusual character, an ex-docker who listened to Pavarotti and read books on Zen. He had a good deal of common sense and he'd been around.

There was no doubt that Terry was a winner. He only wanted winners in his stable, and I could live with that. I wasn't in boxing to be an also-ran. If I stuck with Terry I reckoned I had a good chance of getting to the top. And if you don't get to the top in boxing, there's an awful lot of bottom.

Terry told me I was going to have to work bloody hard. I wouldn't be ready for a proper title fight for at least five or six years. That made sense to me. I looked around the heavyweight division and most of the successful boxers were well into their twenties. This was going to be a long campaign.

But before the show got rolling, I made an awful ricket. I forgot to tell Terry I had already made an agreement with another manager. That might sound daft to most people – and it certainly sounded daft to Terry – but I was still getting used to the boxing business. In my naivety, I thought you could have more than one person looking after your affairs.

Burt McCarthy was a south London businessman whose family were big noises in the fight game. Freddy Rix introduced me to him while I was still an amateur. Burt used to come around to Barmouth Road in his flash Rolls-Royce, wearing his fancy jewellery. I was impressed. I'd never seen such wealth. So, before I'd even thrown a punch in training for Terry, before I'd even got my professional licence, Burt and I came to an understanding about my career.

Burt thought we had a legally binding contract, that I would sign with him when I turned pro. Then Terry came along. Without thinking any more of it, I signed with him. When I told Terry about Burt, all hell broke loose.

'What were you thinking of, Frank?' he said. 'I can't believe you were so stupid.' It was the first time I'd seen him lose his temper.

He and Mickey were in charge. They knew best. I should be grateful for their help. All I had to do was get in the ring and fight. Then we'd all make loads of money together.

I was confused. I was the guy taking the risks. I was the guy selling the tickets. I thought I was employing them. But I accepted what they said and I got on with my career. What choice did I have? I had to trust somebody.

They saw Burt off for the time being. But the legal row would drag on for years. It was my first nasty experience in boxing. I thought it would be fairly straightforward: you fight, you get paid, you win a title, you retire, you live happily ever after. I was finding out the hard way that boxing is more complicated than that. And over the years I would become slightly paranoid. I'd leave behind all the people with their fine advice. In the end, I'd trust only myself. And God.

The start of the eighties was a great time to be in boxing. The sport had a much bigger profile then. A lot of the papers still had specialist boxing writers, and men like Hugh McIlvanney and Colin Hart were household names. It was also big on television, where Harry Carpenter and Reg Gutteridge were stars. We only had the three channels – and boxing only had three organising bodies. People knew who the champions were – the game seemed to be more import- ant to more people than it is today.

Terry, Mickey and their friends pretty much ruled big-time boxing in this country – this was just before Frank Warren arrived. Mickey was on first-name terms with all the promoters and television executives here and in America. He had been making big deals for a long time and could mix it with the likes of Don King. The United States was where the real money was, where the champions were. If you wanted a world title, you'd have to go over there and get it. Over here, Mickey had a deal with the BBC, which was why the Canning Town fighters were so well known. You can't buy the sort of publicity we had.

To be honest, I wasn't really a fan of Mickey Duff's to start with. He was a great deal-maker, probably the best, but he was a bit too concerned about being in charge for my liking. He was the boss. He didn't want to hear any other side of the story, and I didn't bother to give him one. Not at first, anyway. Terry used to stand up to him, although Mickey usually got his way. Terry, as my manager, had final say on who I fought; but Mickey, who had been around boxing since the late forties, could pick up the phone and get an opponent at a moment's notice. They worked brilliantly together. They had a matchmaker in New York, Johnny Bos. His job was to scout around for my next victim. People used to call Johnny the Gravedigger, which was a bit harsh. He did manage to find some soft touches. If there is such a thing. Both Mickey and Terry had a good idea what purse the other fighter would settle for – and how good or bad he was. Mickey was a tremendous judge of a fighter, a great matchmaker in his own right. In fact, that was his first job in boxing after he retired as a fighter, making the matches down at the old Manor Road Baths. He was a hard, hard man, who'd grown up in adversity.

Maurice Prager was his real name. No one knows for sure why he changed his name to Mickey Duff. Some say it was after a character of that name in a gangster movie; but there was also a real-life New York gangster called Mickey Duffy. Anyway, our Mickey was a Jewish refugee from Eastern Europe who'd arrived in London before the Second World War. He couldn't speak a word of English until he was ten. His father didn't want him to box. He wanted him to be a rabbi. Mickey was determined to be a fighter, so he had to change his name. He always says he wouldn't have paid to watch himself – he was that ugly as a boxer. He had around sixty fights and won nearly all of them. He retired after less than two years – and he still wasn't twenty. 'I knew there was more money to be made outside the ring than in it,' he used to say. How right can you be.

From the moment he got up in the morning, until he went

to sleep at night, Mickey Duff knew a hundred different ways to make money. He was one serious cat.

Mickey and Terry saw straight away that I had the sort of personality that could make me a star. I was fine with that. I did what I was told. And the press decided I was a happy, smiling black dude from Wandsworth. Which was true, although there was more to me than that. I could crack the one-liners, smile for the cameras. But I knew I couldn't rely on gimmicks to make it. What I did have – and it's what all fighters dream of – was an almighty punch. There aren't a lot of world heavyweight titles won on points or fancy boxing. When it comes down to it, it's all about knockouts.

You can't invent power. You can work on what you've got but if the genes aren't right you'll struggle to knock the cream off a coffee. When I throw a big right hand that lands properly, I can feel the electricity down to my socks. You can imagine – or maybe you can't – what it's like to be on the other end of it.

The big smile and the big punch – that's what Terry and the others were buying into. But the story was almost over before it started.

5

Stoned in Colombia

OF ALL THE DUMB THINGS THAT HAVE HAPPENED TO ME, THE TRIP to Bogotá is right up there. It's still hard to believe I got away with it.

I was so excited about turning pro. What could stop me now? I was nineteen and I just wanted to get on with it. First, I had to go through the formalities. To get your boxing licence you have to pass a strict medical, but I couldn't imagine there'd be any problems. I was as fit as a flea.

That's not what the doctor told me.

I was short-sighted in my right eye, he said. Under the rules of the British Boxing Board of Control, fighters need perfect vision, and you can't argue with that. It's the most dangerous sport in the world, especially if you can't see the punches coming. For anyone else less than perfect sight is not much of a problem. But you can hardly box in glasses. So, when the board doctor told me I wasn't fit to box I was shattered.

Everything I'd dreamt about, all the training, the titles,

the talk in the papers, they meant nothing now. Boxing had saved me. It used up the energy that once got me into trouble. It taught me respect. And discipline. It gave me a purpose in life. From the day my father bought me my first pair of gloves, I knew what I wanted. At Oak Hall I started to believe in myself. I'd been the youngest ever ABA heavyweight champion. And now it looked like a life on the building sites. Or worse. A lot of my old mates had drifted into street crime and I definitely didn't want to go down that road.

Terry and I discussed the options. We hadn't got off to the best of starts with the Burt McCarthy fiasco, and now there was this crisis. But Terry didn't panic. He and Mickey said I would have to have an operation. 'There's no other way, Frank,' Terry said. 'You can't box with a dodgy eye.'

We went to see a man who would play a big part in my career, David McLeod, a specialist at the Moorfields Eye Hospital in central London. Terry knew David already: the year before, he'd operated on Maurice Hope's eye and saved his career. He told me I had a rare weakness in my retina.

'There is a new operation that could fix your eye, Frank,' he said. I hung on his every word. 'The only thing is, there's no guarantee it will work.' I didn't care. It was the only shot I had. Then he told me there were only two places in the world where I could get it done: Moscow, or Bogotá.

Moscow I'd heard of. Bogotá? Didn't have a clue. But I'd have gone to the moon to save my career. Terry and Mickey had no doubts. Bogotá might have been the drugs capital of the world, but they didn't fancy Moscow. It was still in the old Soviet days and there would have been a mountain of red tape. I was going to Colombia as soon as they could get me on a plane.

'You'll have to go on your own, Frank,' Terry said, 'because I can't afford to take the time off. I've got a lot of other boxers here to look after. But don't worry. A friend of ours will meet you at the airport. He'll make sure you're looked after.

'Everything will be fine, Frank. If you can get over this, you'll be able to handle anything in boxing. This is only going to take maybe a couple of months. You won't be fighting for a world title for at least five or six years. You and I know we're in it for the long term. That's the way I've always done things. It's tough, but it's the best way.'

I can't say I was thrilled. Patience wasn't my strong suit. Worse, I felt totally alone. If I didn't get my licence – and there was no guarantee I would – that would be it for me; Terry and Mickey could always find another prospect.

I'd hardly ever been out of the country, to Dublin and Boulogne, in fact. Now I was going halfway round the world. On my own. To a place I'd never heard of. Where they didn't speak much English – and I certainly didn't speak any Spanish. I was also putting my future in the hands of a doctor I'd never met. I would have liked Dr McLeod to do the operation but I trusted his advice. He wasn't the sort of man to send me on a wild-goose chase. I gritted my teeth and got on with it.

The last thing Terry told me before I left was to be on my guard. He said Bogotá was where Bobby Moore was arrested in 1970. England had stopped off there on the way to the World Cup, and the police had accused Moore of stealing jewellery.

'They'll stitch you up as soon as look at you, Frank,' Terry said. Anyway, there was no turning back now.

I touched down in Bogotá in February of 1981. I was a long way from home and very nervous. As I came through customs I looked around for the guy who was supposed to meet me. He wasn't there. A great start. All I had was my bag and a piece of paper with a couple of telephone numbers on it. One was for the hospital and, after a few comedy hand signals, someone helped me work out where I was trying to go. They called me a taxi and I went straight there.

At the hospital life started getting a little less complicated. Terry's contact, a travel agent, sent a friend called Helen to find me. She took me to his house and I stayed with him for a couple of days. His family were very nice, spoke English, and I felt comfortable again. Just as I was making myself at home, I had to book in at the hospital.

Any operation on the eye is serious. You don't have to be a scientist to know that. But mine was a new form of treatment. I felt like a guinea pig. Don't get me wrong. Terry and Mickey had paid out £5,000 for me to be here and I was grateful. But then they were always telling me I should be grateful. I wasn't in the best of moods.

The doctor, Professor José Ignacio Barraquer, had to reshape my cornea. I was given a local anaesthetic and then he cut into my eye, stitching it up as he went. He kept it all in place with some sort of superglue. That's probably not how Professor Barraquer would describe it, but that was basically it. It only took twenty minutes. Recovering wouldn't be so simple.

The Bruno brood: with (*from left*) Michael, Faye, Angela and Joan.

Me, aged two.

(*Below left*) My dad, Robert Bruno.

The Oak Hall cricket team: I'm the second from the right, a thirteen-year-old England test bowler in the making.

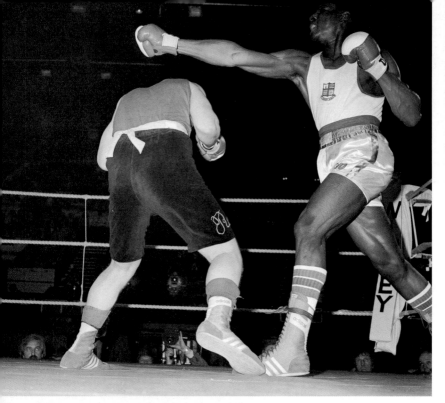

My last amateur fight, against Rudi
Pika, Wembley Arena, 2 May 1980.
I'm about to become the youngest
ever ABA heavyweight champion.
Des Lynam's there at ringside.

Me and Terry Lawless
– we had some good times.

Me and my mother, Lynette.

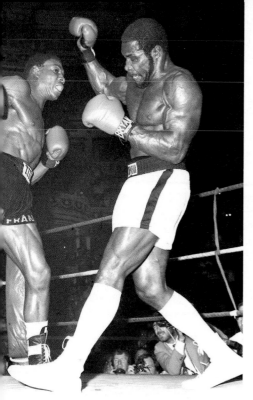

'Jumbo' Cummings, Royal Albert Hall, October 1983 – I dodged a bullet that night.

Me and Harry Carpenter – we made a great double act, even if Harry's not too keen on my tie.

Just when it was all going so well, Wembley Arena, 13 May 1984. I'm in control against 'Bonecrusher' Smith here ... but in the last round he nailed me.

On the ropes: (*above*) I put Gerrie Coetzee flat on his back, Wembley Arena, 4 March 1986; (*below*) four months later at Wembley Stadium Tim Witherspoon gives me the same treatment

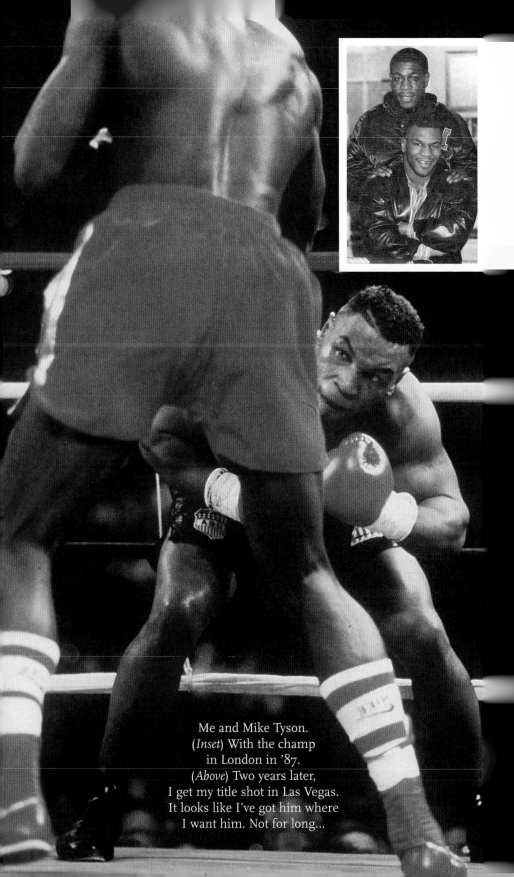

Me and Mike Tyson.
(*Inset*) With the champ
in London in '87.
(*Above*) Two years later,
I get my title shot in Las Vegas.
It looks like I've got him where
I want him. Not for long...

Taking care of business: (*above*) working the speedball at Canning Town; (*below*) all smiles with my promoter, Mickey Duff; (*right*) laughing it up with Lenny Henry in *Romeo and Juliet*, 1985.

(*Left*) Me and my girls, Nicola and Rachel.

Back in the picture:
I've just knocked out Jose Ribalta,
Wembley, 22 April 1992.

Henri Brandman delivers a writ to
Lennox Lewis at our pre-fight press
conference. We dropped the writ,
but I thought Lennox had dissed me.
We don't have a problem now.

The real fight: me and Lennox,
Cardiff, 1 October 1993.

Stand by your man:
(*above*) me and Laura after
the Lewis fight; (*left*) and
on our wedding day,
5 February 1990.

When the juice wore off, I felt as if I'd been hit in the head by a runaway train. But the doctor was thrilled with the result. And that cheered me up no end. He had saved my career. 'You should be able to start training again in a few months,' he said. 'But you've got to be very careful, Mr Bruno. The stitches can't be disturbed. The eye is a very delicate instrument.'

I wanted to get on the first plane home, but my next stop was a bed and breakfast somewhere in the city. I arrived with my head bandaged like some Egyptian mummy and I was told I had to lie on my bed as still as I could – for the rest of my stay. That's a long time for a boxer to be flat on his back.

I knew there was no way I could keep still for six weeks. I'd never been able to keep still for six minutes. Still, I got through the first day in reasonable shape. The people who ran the place were very friendly but they spoke hardly any English. So I spent the whole day staring at the ceiling. I've never been one for reading books, and there was only *Bonanza* and *Ironside* – in Spanish – on the TV. There were two other patients from the hospital staying there, an old man from El Salvador and a young Venezuelan, and we played a bit of chess. I did OK. I'd learnt the game at Oak Hall. But I knew this wasn't going to last.

I had to get out. The first time I went for a walk, I came across a guy waving a gun around. I don't know if he was waving it at me, and I didn't wait to find out. I ran back to my hostel as fast as I could, holding my hand to my bandaged eye.

Pretty soon I got to know the neighbourhood. One day I was taking a taxi into town when three guys wearing masks jumped in. This is it, I thought: shot dead in a cab. What I didn't know was the taxi was a *'collectivo'*, which meant it could pick up more than one passenger. My new friends had handkerchiefs around their mouths because of the pollution. Close one.

Still, as the days dragged on, I was bored out of my mind. On one of my walks, I met a guy near the hostel who said he knew where I could get some dope. 'Right,' I said, 'where do I go?' He took me to a house in one of the less fancy parts of Bogotá – which was saying something. The best way to get there was by bus, a bit of a challenge for a one-eyed boy from Wandsworth who didn't speak the language. Things got better: we broke down going up a hill. I was the biggest guy on the bus so I had to get out and push. After what seemed like hours, I found the place. Buying dope is a straightforward business in any part of the world. You come to a price and pay the money. Simple.

Then things got tricky. When I got back to the hostel, I met some guys who invited me to a barbecue. They weren't just serving hamburgers. It seemed word had got out that there was a new punter in town. I might have been a biggish name back in Britain, but they had no idea who I was. All they knew was I wasn't from Bogotá. I was on my own, a long way from home, and they went to work on me.

'We've got someone we'd like you to meet, Frank,' my new friends said. 'Very nice guy. Big house. Lots of girls and champagne. He's a very powerful man, very influential. A good man to know if you're going to enjoy your stay, Frank.'

It was probably stupid of me – in fact, there's no probably about it – but I agreed to go. I was young, life was a bit of a laugh – and I was going stir-crazy. Anything to get out of the house. I didn't realise the risk I was running – to my eye, maybe even to my life.

As I sat in the back of the limousine it dawned on me, and I wondered how Terry could have let me come here by myself. We'd been driving for a little while. I looked out the window. The houses were bigger, the streets cleaner. And then we pulled up in front of one of the grandest houses in the neighbourhood.

'Listen, Frank,' my host said when we got inside. 'We'd like you to do us a little favour. Dope is just chicken feed. We deal mainly in cocaine: LA, New York, London, all the big cities. That's where the money is. But we've got to get the stuff there first.'

I could see what was coming, and I was getting a bit twitchy.

'Yeah? What's that got to do with me?'

'Well, Frank, you'll be going back to London soon. We'd like you to deliver a little package for us. It'll be easy – no hassles. We have people at the other end who'll make sure you get through with the stuff. All you have to do is keep it close to you – very close to you.' He gave me a piece of paper with a London address on it. 'Just make sure it gets there. Easy as that.'

'I don't think so, sir. My thing is puff. I've never had anything to do with cocaine. I've never even seen the stuff. I don't want to get involved. If it's all the same to you, sir.'

There was a bit of a pause. He looked to his friends and said something in Spanish. All the time, he was smiling.

'Come on, Frank. We're your friends. You'd be doing us a big favour. And this is a dangerous town. A lot of crazy things happen to people, if you understand us.'

I did. He might have thought I was an easy mark, but I didn't fancy walking around with half a pound of white powder up my backside. As politely as I could, I kept saying, 'No, thanks.' I was a big, strong young boxer. I knew I could look after myself – but not with only one good eye. I was flying by the seat of my pants. I just had to hold my nerve and see if he backed off.

I have to say my new friends were entirely charming. That was why they were dangerous, though. Nothing is like it seems in Bogotá. It's a jungle. Most of the people are hungry and desperate; a few at the top are extremely ruthless. Not too many middle-class people here, from what I could see. These guys weren't high society. They were Colombian cocaine dealers. People get shot if they do the wrong thing in this sort of company.

I had one card to play: I might not be known at all in Bogotá, but I was a champion amateur boxer backed by some of the most powerful people in the business. If they got nasty, my name would be all over the papers back home. I hinted at this without trying to stir things up. I think they got the message. Soon enough, they stopped talking about coke deals. I think they found me amusing. This might have been the start of my acting career.

It sounds crazy, but I figured now this was just one big adventure. Really, I should have been lying in a darkened room letting my eye heal; instead, I was mixing with big-time drug dealers. It lasted maybe an hour – the longest sixty minutes of my life.

I thought I'd seen a few things on the streets of south London. This was something else. These guys meant business. They weren't happy, but I didn't think they were going to put a bullet in my head for not taking their cocaine back home. My new friends had different plans.

'Frank, if you get to fight in the States, it would be nice if you could, you know, maybe introduce us to some people. It would be good to get to know some of the big names in the business. There's a huge market there for us. And there's plenty of fighters who already buy our stuff. If you do make it, Frank, you won't forget your friends . . . will you?'

'No, sir.'

I didn't know then how persistent these guys could be. For years afterwards, if I was in a big fight, they'd be in touch. They'd write me a postcard or leave a message at the hotel. 'Frank, we'd like to talk.' I didn't think they'd ever do anything stupid, so I ignored them. In the end, they stopped calling. The funny thing is, I didn't really dislike them. They were serious gangsters, but you take people as you find them. I always took the view that what I didn't know couldn't kill me.

My eye was slowly getting better. Soon enough I'd be home and, if everything went well, the board would give me my licence. I couldn't wait to get back in the ring.

6

Laura

IT WAS A BIT HARD TO MISS LAURA MOONEY. AND SHE DIDN'T miss me when she pinched my big backside at a roller-skating rink in Battersea. It's a true story even though it's been told so often it sounds like a fairy tale. It was the summer of 1981, not long after I'd got back from Colombia. Laura was twenty-one and full of cheek, and I was not yet twenty and 'out fishing'.

Our relationship grew slowly. I liked her attitude and the fact that she had no idea who I was. She told a newspaper a couple of years after we met that 'it wasn't exactly love at first sight'. Before our first Christmas, she was pregnant and we'd started our adventure together.

It's hard to describe the feeling of being a father for the first time. When Nicola arrived I was as proud as any man on the planet. She was just so beautiful – still is, in fact. When she arrived it made me even more determined to succeed as a fighter, to give her every chance in life. Nicola lit up all our lives. To this day, she's a rock for me, always there when I need her.

Laura's family were thrilled for us too, and I know my mother was proud – even if she would have preferred us to get married before we started a family. She's always been very traditional.

For the first six months or so my mother made space for the three of us alongside everyone else at Barmouth Road. It was cosy, to say the least, but we made the best of it. There were my three sisters, my brother Michael, Mum, Nicola, Laura and yours truly. At least we were never short of a babysitter. When we could afford it, Laura and I would leave Nicola with Mum or the sisters and head out for a quiet meal in the local area. Otherwise we'd stay in and watch TV. Exciting, eh? Apart from my little escapade in Bogotá, I've never been one for the bright lights, believe it or not; besides, we didn't have the money. I'm sure that millions of young couples across the country start their lives together the same way. You're just glad to be in each other's company and you do without the frills. It's no great sacrifice.

Laura came from west London – Hammersmith, near where I was born – and didn't stand on ceremony. She was a very good talker, was Laura, which suited me. I was happy to give her a good listening to. We hit it off without any problems. She didn't care if I was black or white, rich or poor. And, at that stage of my life, I didn't have a brass farthing.

Life seemed so simple. I'd got out of Colombia in one piece. All I had to do now was buckle down and turn myself into a good pro. I could hardly wait for my first fight. I didn't know it at the time, but life would never be so uncomplicated again.

I was up every morning at five to go running in Battersea Park, then home for breakfast, and to see Laura before she headed off to work – she was a nursery nurse. After that, it was off to the Brixton branch of the Lonsdale sports shop, where I'd try to make myself useful behind the counter. Bert Hamilton, my sister Faye's partner, had fixed me up with the job through Bernard Hart, who ran Lonsdale.

Later, I'd meet up with Lloyd Honeyghan and tube it up to Canning Town to the gym. We didn't always pay the required fare, but we were young and didn't have a care in the world. Lloyd used to make those journeys a laugh.

One day, though, wasn't so funny. I'd gone up to Canning Town on my own. I'd brought my skates with me to make the journey from the tube to the gym quicker. I was skating along the platform at Stratford station when four skinheads spotted me and started in with a lot of racist abuse. As they came towards me, I got ready to look after myself – not the easiest thing to do when you're on roller skates. I feared the worst. Then, from the other platform, I heard someone shout: 'Oi, leave it out, you lot!' It was like Batman had arrived. This total stranger dashed over the bridge and joined in on my side as we swapped words with these nutters. There was some minor argy-bargy – I didn't contribute much on my mobile shoes – and the guys ran off.

'Thanks very much for that, mate,' I said to the stranger.

'No problem. You've got to be a bit careful around here. Anyway, Cass Pennant's the name. Glad to help.'

Over the years, Cass became a good friend, and he would

be there again when I needed him most. He wasn't exactly an angel – he ran with a pretty hard crew of West Ham fans. Years later, he would write a book about his days as a football hooligan. But he was OK to me, and I was grateful for his help. You learn something every day on the street.

We had some great times in Terry's gym. We worked hard, but we knew how to have a good time too. I'm a bit of a loner by nature, but you couldn't help but get involved in the banter at the Royal Oak. It was a classic East End gym, tucked away above a pub in a run-down part of town and teeming with characters. It was also a wonderful place for me to get rid of my pent-up energy. All my life the gym has been my refuge, a place where I can get loose by sweating up, letting the punches go, pushing my body to the limit. It gives you a rush that's hard to describe and it gets you hooked.

Before you even get to throw a punch, there's the running to do. The days I didn't run in Battersea Park, I did five to seven miles in the forest at Hainault. It was better when I had company. Sometimes I was lucky enough to be joined by one of the fittest boxers I've ever met, the featherweight Jim McDonnell. Jim is a good friend to this day. He's about half my size, and I had to really work to stay up with him. It was insurance, miles on the clock for those tough later parts of a fight when you need all the stamina you can stuff into your system. For a big man like me, it wasn't easy, but I pushed myself all the way, every day.

Jim trains fanatically, even now. He was responsible for getting Danny Williams into the shape of his life before he knocked out Mike Tyson. But back in the early days, Jim had his own ambitions, like so many boxers at the Royal Oak. It's what made it such a good place to train. There was a feeling that this was a place where you could turn yourself into someone special.

As you went in, you'd see Charlie Magri working on the pads. Terry would be talking tactics with the trainers. Everywhere you looked there'd be champions, present and future: Maurice Hope, Jim Watt, Ray Cattouse, who were the stars of the day; then there was Charlie, who'd win the world flyweight title, Lloyd, who'd be champion at welterweight, and Kirkland Laing, who should have been. When Lloyd and Kirkland sparred, it was magic, better than many world title fights. If Terry had had his wits about him, he would have charged us to watch it.

Jimmy Tibbs was my trainer. He worked with Frank Black, who also looked after my conditioning. I'd been lucky to spend those six months in Highgate with George Francis, but I knew I was in good hands at the Royal Oak. Jimmy and Frank were two of the best in the business. Frank was a wise Irishman who sometimes came to Mass with me on Sundays. Jimmy had been a respected middleweight who got into a bit of trouble outside the ring. He did ten years after trying to settle a family argument without a lot of diplomacy. Jimmy came out a reformed man and is now a born-again Christian. He was a fine trainer but six years after I started at the Royal Oak he fell out with the gym and joined Frank Warren. That's when I picked up again with George, who would be with me up to the end.

The Royal Oak was a wonderful place to swap stories, some of them true. I was surrounded by a collection of hard-core boxing characters and about to set off on a grand adventure. I loved it straight away, it was like a private club for scoundrels and good guys. And who should I see training when I got there but my old mate from Oak Hall, Gunter Roomes. There's no getting away from some people.

I don't suppose Laura was thrilled that I was going to earn my living punching people in the head, but she didn't make a thing of it. If that's what you want to do, she said, I'm with you all the way. At first it wasn't easy to fit my boxing and training in around my work at the sports shop. It was a long round trip: Wandsworth, Brixton, Canning Town, Wandsworth. By the time I got back to Laura and Nicola, I was knackered. But it was only for a few months. Now that Terry was giving me a decent sub, I could give up the job in Brixton. I was pretty much a full-time professional athlete.

Boxing wasn't just a hobby to me; it was my way out, a way out for Laura and Nicola too, for a better life. I had no complaints about my upbringing, but I wanted the best I could achieve for my family, and I wasn't going to do it earning a few bob selling running shoes in a shop in Brixton. I was going to do it with my fists.

There wasn't much glamour attached to training. But, if I was going to box for a living, if I was going to make it, I'd have to give it my heart and soul. That wasn't a problem for me. I was never afraid of hard work. Besides, I knew I had the tools for it. I wasn't going to waste my power on a building site. I put my growing body through the mill.

One of the secrets of getting fit to fight lies in an exercise that involves no punching at all. It's on the floor that you build the foundations for everything else, turning the top half of your body into a solid chunk of muscle. I did thou-sands of sit-ups, press-ups, chin-ups – all the basic exercises that work your midriff. Then there were the twists and stretches to stay supple. It was second nature to me, as it is to all boxers. If you don't get the basics right, forget it. Fighters have been using the same routine for hundreds of years.

To give yourself the best chance in the gym, you also have to eat well. As a heavyweight, of course, I never had to worry about getting down to a certain weight – like boxers in the lighter divisions – but I still had to choose the right diet. You get nowhere on junk food. It clogs up your system and gives you no energy. I was lucky that I grew up eating my mother's West Indian cooking. It was full of the right stuff – chicken and fish, lots of rice and pasta, the energy foods that keep you going. And I had an enormous appetite.

As well as the hard work in the gym, you have to clock up the miles on the road. I liked to run early in the morning, when the air is clean and fresh, free of car fumes. I loved it because it was so healthy. I could put my cares behind me as Jim and I pounded through the forest, thinking of nothing but the ground in front of us. I could feel my body responding to the workload, feel my heart working away as I got fitter and fitter.

Sparring was like a present after the hard work. I loved learning the skills of boxing – the way to open up an oppo-nent, to push my lead through his guard, make him drop his gloves, then deliver a right hand or a left hook. Jimmy knew all the moves, making me shift my weight from my knees up to my hips, through my shoulders and all the way down my arms to my fists, turning them at the last minute for full impact.

Everyone has to learn combinations. You work on those in front of the mirror, shadow-boxing: left, right, hook, jab, uppercut. Left, right, hook, jab, uppercut. After a while, one follows the other like night follows day. You throw them without thinking.

You have to deal with the punches coming the other way, of course. So, when you jab, you learn to bring your arm straight back to where it started to cover your jaw. It works like a piston, in and out, in and out. At the same time, you try to move your upper body and your head, making them sway automatically so that you're not a sitting target. You have to shift your feet without thinking, getting close enough to throw a punch or sliding to the side for a better angle, or backing out of range when your opponent is looking to land a counter. And all the time you have to keep your balance.

Over the years, you turn yourself into a fighting machine. It's a bit like driving a racing car. You put the key in the ignition and let the engine go. But, if you don't want to crash, you have to concentrate every second. The other guy is trying to do exactly the same. You have to anticipate what he might do next. Some fighters do this by instinct, others have to learn it by repetition. I put the hours in, day after day, to make it as natural as I could. I was never going to be a fancy boxer, but I did get the basics right. I kept it nice and simple. My aim was to get into place to land my big punches as cleanly as I could. It sounds easy but, believe me, it's not. Boxing is one of the toughest sports in the world to do properly.

When I could afford it, I bought an old Ghia, a step up on my first car. I thought it was a bit of a luxury. I wasn't earning a fortune – in fact, Laura was the main breadwinner – and money was tight. But it was getting crowded at Barmouth Road, and we knew sooner or later we'd have to move out. We decided on Hornchurch in Essex. For a start, it would be closer to the gym. I was going to the States with Terry, Mickey and Lloyd for a couple of months, so Laura would have to sort out the move by herself – luckily, she was a good organiser. I would come to appreciate how good she was at looking after my affairs.

For now, Terry was in charge. He was very upbeat and reckoned there would be some great nights down the road. As Terry had said before, he and Mickey viewed me as an investment. They were prepared to gamble by taking me to the States as part of my boxing education – and I hadn't even thrown a punch for pay. It sounded fair enough to me.

Life was looking good – but it's never as straightforward as it seems. When Laura, Nicola and I made the move to Essex, I heard about the sniping behind our backs, about the white girl and the black boxer moving off to a posh house. Well, it wasn't that posh, for a start. It was a nice, comfortable place, with a few bedrooms. We hadn't exactly moved into Buckingham Palace. But that didn't stop some people. They couldn't hide their envy – or was it something more evil than that?

I've never understood racism, never understood why people just can't accept others for what they are. I know it's only a few people who have a twisted view of other races, and I feel sorry for them. Maybe they thought I was being handed life on a plate. They saw a young ABA champion who hadn't even had a professional fight. What was so special about him? And what was wrong with living in Wandsworth?

Nothing at all, of course. But it was our life. I've always liked Essex and I felt comfortable the moment we moved in. And this was going to be where Nicola started growing up.

Before I could get my career going, though, I had to pass another medical. As far as we were concerned, the Bogotá operation had been a complete success. The boxing board weren't convinced. They still couldn't decide if it was safe for me to box. The board's doctor, Adrian Whiteson, said that, even if they did give me my licence, I'd have to have regular check-ups on my eye. I couldn't understand the hold-up. It was driving Terry round the bend too. 'The board don't get much wrong,' he told me. 'But they should think again on this one. Your eye is safe as houses.'

Terry explained it to me. He said that until the early eighties, everyone thought short-sighted boxers were a liability. One good hit around the head and they'd end up with a detached retina. But what the board didn't recognise was the new operation had made my eye even stronger. Terry reckoned they should have known that. It was one of the few times I saw him lose his temper.

'So, what do I do now?' I said.

'Nothing you can do, Frank, except keep on training – and waiting and hoping.'

And that's what I did. Seven days a week for another long year. Sweating it up Canning Town. I probably worked as hard then as I did preparing for my world title fights. Thank God for the heavy bag. That's where I took out my frustrations. Without it, I might have put my fist through the nearest wall. As the months went by and we still didn't have an answer from the board, I just kept working. That convinced

Terry how committed I was. If I could keep going when the wheels were coming off, the least he could do was keep faith in me. It was an important stage of our relationship. It was all about trust.

Finally, eighteen months after I'd left the amateurs, the board gave me my licence. It was the best news I had ever received. It might as well have been the world title itself. It was now up to me and I couldn't wait to get at it. Terry and Mickey quickly set up my first fight: St Patrick's Day 1982, at the Royal Albert Hall, against Lupe Guerra of North Platte, Nebraska. Surely nothing else could go wrong . . . It did.

One day I came home from the gym and told Laura we had a little problem. He came from south London and his name was Burt McCarthy. I'd almost forgotten about him.

'I have the only contract signed by Frank Bruno,' Burt told the press, 'and it's lodged with the British Boxing Board of Control. I'm his manager. Under no circumstances will there be any prospect of Frank appearing at the Albert Hall.'

You can imagine how angry Terry and Mickey were. They quickly arranged their own press conference. 'I've done everything according to the regulations,' Terry said. 'We've been together for two years now and that's how it will stay.'

So just before the fight, they went to court. Now it was the lawyers' turn to argue the toss. Burt's brief, a Mr Sparrow, told the court my opponent was too experienced for me. He said the fight could ruin my career and my reputation. Maybe Mr Sparrow should have been a boxing manager. He sounded as if he'd been in the game all his life.

Our lawyer went for a different angle. 'At the time of

signing,' he said, 'Frank was training in Mr Lawless's gym. He was of limited intelligence and education and signed the document after Terry Lawless was run down and Burt McCarthy was built up.'

I was the one who felt like he was being 'run down'. It wasn't nice to be told you were of 'limited intelligence and education' – especially with all the newspaper guys there.

I thought it would all be over quickly. The judge said McCarthy and I didn't have a contract. The fight was on. But Burt wasn't finished. He would take this through the courts for another five years. Apparently I was a prize worth fighting over.

Mr Sparrow shouldn't have worried. Lupe Guerra might not have been the best heavyweight in North Platte, Nebraska.

7

'They Won't all be that Easy'

A HUNDRED AND FORTY-ONE SECONDS INTO MY FIRST PROFESSIONAL fight, I threw the perfect right. It travelled maybe a couple of feet and landed cleanly on Lupe Guerra's jaw. Ten seconds later, North Platte's finest was being helped up from the canvas and led back to his corner. My night's work was over. It had taken two years, an operation on my eye and a lot of legal hassles, but I was on my way. And the Albert Hall swelled with the sound of my name for the first time: 'Broo-no! Broo-no!'

I'd been dreaming about the fight for weeks, trying to ignore the Burt McCarthy case, trying to be professional. It seemed like I'd been waiting for this night for ever. I had so much energy stored up I had no idea how it was going to come out. I couldn't be sure if I'd go to pieces or keep it together. I'd never been so nervous.

On the long walk from the dressing room I tried to ignore

the crowd, but it was impossible. As Terry and I worked our way up to the corner, I heard my friends at ringside screaming encouragement. I was shaking. 'Stay calm, Frank,' Terry said. 'Keep it simple. Work behind your jab and wait for an opening.' I nodded and sweated. I'd had twenty-one amateur fights but they meant nothing here. This was the real thing.

Smaller, fatter, older – that's the sort of opponent you want when you're starting out. Lupe qualified on at least the first and last counts. He was 14st 7lb, a stone lighter than me. He was certainly more experienced, and had won seventeen of his twenty-three fights. But for the last four years these had been around Omaha, Nebraska. Believe me, it's not the boxing capital of the world. Also, he'd been knocked out in five of his previous seven fights. There was no getting away from it: he was a soft touch. He went over early and easy from a punch I can't remember throwing. Moments later, I put him down for a count of eight with an uppercut. I finished him off with a left–right.

I was happy to win but it wasn't much of a test. It was a public workout to show me off to the punters, but they'd need something better than this to keep coming back. After all, this was the Albert Hall. Most novices start at small venues like the York Hall in Bethnal Green. This was the red-carpet treatment from the off. A year before I'd been working on a building site; now I was centre stage at one of the most famous venues in the history of boxing. Terry, Mickey and their partners had shown they could deliver on their promises. And I'd proved I could deliver my end of the bargain.

As I looked out over the ropes at the thousands of faces, I felt special, but a little confused. They'd come to see if the youngest ever ABA champion could cut it as a pro. Would I really be the heavyweight champion of the world, like my brother Michael used to tell me? Or would I end up like a lot of fighters, broke and forgotten?

In some ways, what I was doing seemed ridiculous. There were all these people I didn't know cheering my win, and sitting on his stool in the other corner was a beaten-up Mexican, a total stranger, looking like he wanted to get on the first plane back to Omaha. To this day, I've never found out what happened to him.

I had nothing against the guy. How could I? It was my job to get him out of the way. As a fighter, you have to ignore any personal feelings. You have to be cold and unfeeling about your work. Boxers know about these pressures – they can do funny things to your head. I didn't hate any of my opponents. In fact, I quite liked some of them. But you can't think like that before a fight. It's strictly business.

In the amateurs boxing is more straightforward. There's no showbiz. The audience is part of the fight, because amateur boxing is a small, closed world. It's very tribal. The people shouting your name are your friends and family. The ones you don't know are shouting for the other guy. You're more likely to be evenly matched; your opponent might even be a friend.

As a pro, unless it's a title fight, you choose your opponent – as long as your people are paying the money. It's not a fix, it's the way it is. Terry was a cautious man and he wasn't going to take risks with his hot property. Mickey wouldn't have been too pleased if he had. No manager is going to put his prospect in with a dangerous opponent early in his career.

I wanted to put on a good show for the fans – maybe I'd have liked someone better than Guerra first up – but boxers have to learn their trade in public. Some writers don't like it. They reckon it's a sham, that fight fans are being hood-winked. But I don't think it's entirely like that. Hard-core followers of the sport know how it works. Nobody expected my first opponent to be Larry Holmes or Mike Weaver, the champions of the day. What they didn't want was boxing's equivalent of Eddie the Eagle. It had been a reasonable start, no more than that.

How did I feel about it? I did as I was told. Mickey and Terry were wrapping me in cotton wool as they developed me as a brand. They told me to be nice to the reporters – they fed them stories about me, especially the tabloids. I was being sold like a breakfast cereal, but I was fine with that. I wasn't in it just for the glory. I was in it for the money, like they were.

The plan was for me to move up the rankings with as little fuss as possible. Each time you beat someone ahead of you in the list, you should get closer to a title fight, but some-times fighters get lost in the mix. Mickey was great at making sure the guys who run international boxing knew about my progress.

Back then, just before the International Boxing Federation was formed, there were only the two organising bodies – the World Boxing Council and the World Boxing Association. Things were simpler and titles really meant something. I couldn't tell you how many organisations there are today. Nor could most people in boxing. That's why the sport is in such a mess.

'Frank, they won't all be that easy,' Terry told me after the Guerra workout. 'They won't all fall over in a couple of minutes. There are some good heavyweights out there. You have to concentrate on the job. Everything else takes second place when you're getting ready for a fight. You'll have to make a lot of sacrifices.'

The first sacrifice I had to make was my music. I wanted my boom box in the gym. Terry didn't want any sound but gloves on chins, the skipping rope hitting the floor, air coming out of the heavy bag. He was old-fashioned like that. The music of my generation – reggae, house, rock – they meant nothing to him. I was into a lot of the soul artists too – Ray Charles, Aretha Franklin, James Brown. I liked nearly everything, though – even Terry's Pavarotti. We had some groovy guys in that gym, Lloyd Honeyghan, Kirkland Laing, and we kept on at Terry about it.

In the end we won, but the Great Music Debate showed Terry wasn't an easy man to get round. I usually went with the flow because it was in my nature. I was grateful to Terry and I was still learning the business. At the time I thought he knew best – but it was my life, and eventually I'd want it back. For now, though, I'd have to fight the likes of Harvey Steichen.

Harvey – it's not a great name for a fighter. He talked like a fighter, though. 'I'm going to bust your ass,' he told me at the weigh-in. But Harvey came into the ring at Wembley

Arena looking about as dangerous as a pastry cook. He was a couple of inches shorter than me and, at 16st 2lb, nearly a stone heavier. It took me five and a half minutes to finish him off.

The crowd and the critics were kind. Colin Hart said in the *Sun*: 'Bruno showed what a fine boxer he is.' I didn't think I'd proved that much.

I had another eight fights before Christmas and, to be honest, I've had to look up some of their names – they all passed me in a blur. At times I felt like a bouncer throwing guys out of a nightclub.

In April I was back at the Albert Hall. Tom Stevenson, Terry said, had a knockout punch and a decent record, seven wins out of twelve starts. At the weigh-in he looked in shape, but he proved to be just another American passing through. In the round it lasted, Terrified Tom hardly threw a punch. He was counted out on the ring apron after I'd lifted him off his feet with a couple of my best shots. The crowd didn't like it one bit. And, before he went home, the board stopped his $1,000 purse. It was a long way to come for a hiding and then have your wages docked.

I remember going home a little disheartened that night. It was the first time I'd heard booing at one of my fights. It wasn't my fault Stevenson was so bad. Was it Terry's fault, though? No, he said to trust him and I would. He and Mickey had years of experience. I was sure the opponents would get better as my own boxing improved. I had a lot to learn.

I had no problem staying motivated. If anything I was too keen. I threw myself into my training, determined to live up to the expectations people already had of me. I was attracting bigger and bigger crowds. The papers seemed to be running stories on me every week. Even the Americans were taking notice, and one of their big news agencies came to interview me.

Jarvis Astaire fixed up the venue for my next fight, Wembley Arena. This one went four rounds. At least Ron Gibbs tried harder than Tom. Gibbs was from Nevada and, credit to him, he had a bit of class. He was a smart mover and I found it harder to pin him down with my jab. For the first time in my career, I was frustrated. It didn't go exactly to plan. He clipped me a few times with his right-hand counters, then in the fourth with a good uppercut. That seemed to spark my legs and I found a little rhythm. When I let fly with a left hook over his dropped guard, it landed as flush as any punch I'd thrown. Gibbs flew into the ropes. He got up but the referee called it off. I was more relieved than anything else.

Tony Moore had fought fifty-three times before he met me in June, back at the Albert Hall. Tony was from north London and I had sparred with him in the amateurs. I liked him, but this was business, and I don't think he was that keen. I dropped him for a nine-count in the second and it was over. Tony retired; I moved into the British top ten.

Now I was within a few fights of the British title. That would be something, the Lonsdale Belt. It's the most valuable prize in British boxing. People have criticised me for never fighting for my own country's title, but it wasn't that simple. Terry made a cold, hard business decision. My reputation was growing with every fight and other boxers wanted silly money to get in the ring with me. More to the point, Terry didn't think I could learn much fighting local heavyweights. He was right. I was getting tougher work-outs in the gym than I was in front of the paying public. I had to be professional about my career, to go where the money was, to take fights that would build my reputation – especially in America. The papers were starting to grow impa-tient – but Terry ignored them. 'Trust me, Frank,' he'd say. 'We know what we're doing.' After all, I'd only had five fights and ten rounds of boxing.

That July, Terry and Mickey decided I should go to the States for some quality training. We did the rounds of gyms, from New York to Las Vegas. I wanted to go up against the good heavyweights, the guys I might be fighting on my way to a world title. So far, I'd hardly had a glove laid on me. I still wasn't sure how I would react under serious pressure.

First stop was a hotel owned by the WBC heavyweight champion, Larry Holmes. It was moments like these when I realised how much clout Mickey had. He was a regular at most of the big fights in America. He had a place in New York, in the same apartment block as Jim Jacobs, who'd be Mike Tyson's first manager. Jacobs would be a very handy contact in the years to come.

Anyway, here we were in Easton, Pennsylvania, where Holmes was king. He was a very funny man and widely recognised as the best heavyweight in the world. He wouldn't spar with me, though. I don't think he wanted to risk copping a Bruno right hand on the whiskers. But he did give me some good advice. As my Colombian friends had told me, quite a few American fighters were getting into cocaine. 'Stay away from it, Frank,' is what Larry said. I listened then. I wish he'd been around to tell me the same thing years later. In 2000 I found myself in a hotel room in Las Vegas, buying coke from an old acquaintance.

I didn't tell Larry – or many other people, for that matter – that the only drug I did was marijuana. And not that often. I didn't tell Terry and Mickey, either. It wouldn't have gone down well with a couple of straight guys like those two. They were from another time. For all their boxing smarts, they were old-fashioned in a lot of ways. They represented the old cockney spirit, full of wit and not scared of an argument. Rows came and went in our camp as if they were as natural as drinking water. They were usually forgotten before they were over.

Holmes wouldn't spar with me, nor would Michael Spinks, who'd take the IBF title off him three years later, but another champion did. Mike Weaver held the WBA title at the time. He'd lose it that December, but he looked pretty good to me. I held my own against him, and felt I was making real progress.

Next stop was the Catskill Mountains in upstate New York. Mickey wanted me to see where Rocky Marciano had trained. I loved it, working out at Grossinger's, a resort with a training camp attached to it. It went brilliantly.

I sparred with a guy called Jeff Sims, who was the number eleven heavyweight in the world. I bet he thought this young kid from London didn't belong in the same ring as him. It took one solid right hand to change his mind as I sat him on the seat of his pants.

Over dinner that night he told me he'd spent seven years on a chain gang. When he showed me his knife scars, I believed him. He was one of ten children who grew up poor in the Deep South. Jeff had been sent to prison for shooting a man who'd shot him, and he still had four bullets in him. Like a lot of young black men, he started boxing in prison. When he got out he turned professional and kayoed nineteen opponents in a row. He'd slipped a little by the time we met and he never really made it, but I liked him a lot. He was one in a million.

Grossinger's was full of good fighters. A couple of days later, I was mixing it with James 'Quick' Tillis, who'd lost to Mike Weaver in a world title fight. That sparring was invaluable; five years later I'd stop Tillis on my way to my own world title fight.

The Catskills were a great place to train. The air was clean and there were no distractions. From Grossinger's we went to Cus D'Amato's place, where I met Mike Tyson for the first time. He was always hard to figure out. He was vulnerable but, believe me, he was awesome. He had that aura, no question. We sparred a few rounds and I reckoned we finished about equal. Terry was even offered a fight in Los Angeles. He turned it down because he didn't think I was ready.

At least I was moving in good company, getting to see how they trained, the standard of their sparring, some of their moves. After a couple of months, I came home feeling better about my career. Not that the opposition improved much.

That September of 1982, George Scott, a Northern Area champion, lasted a round. I was starting to get restless. In

October, I nipped over to Germany to get away from the local critics for a couple of weeks, and I stopped Ali Lukasa in two rounds. At least he put up a bit of a fight. Somebody mugged him later that night. It's a tough old game.

And so it went. I had another two-rounder, against the Belgian Rudy Gauwe. The German George Butzbach lasted a round. To end the year, I stopped the Puerto Rican Gilberto Acuna back at the Albert Hall. For the second time in my career, the fans booed. I hoped they were booing Acuna, not me. I could only beat what was put in front of me. In ten fights that year, I'd boxed a total of seventeen rounds. Still, *The Ring* magazine made me their Prospect of the Year.

I hoped for better in '83. There was even talk of a fight in January against Joe Bugner, the man who'd ended Henry Cooper's career. Frank Warren said he could put £200,000 on the table. But Terry wasn't happy with a sixty–forty split in Joe's favour, so it never happened. I'd have to wait more than four years to get my hands on Joe.

By now, Nicola had arrived. I had to earn some serious corn – and I needed to go up a level.

But the ordinary opponents just kept coming – and going down. There was a bit of edge in my fight with Stewart Lithgo at the Albert Hall in January. He was a former jumps jockey with a lot of attitude, and another Northern Area champion. It took me four rounds to stop him. 'You're still nothing!' he shouted as he left the ring. Not one of my great nights.

I knocked out the Ugandan Peter Mulindwa in three, stopped Winston Allen in two, Eddie Neilson in three, the tough old American Scott LeDoux in three and Barry Funches in five. I was improving my boxing technique, working on my combinations, but I wanted a more serious examination.

So Terry and Mickey said we were going to the States again. Ever since our first trip I'd wanted to go back. I was getting sick of the Harveys and the Terrified Toms. The real money in the fight game was in America, and Mickey and Terry were doing their best to help me get my hands on it. What I needed was a proper fight. They got me one.

On 9 July, under the chandeliers of the DiVinci Manor, a fancy Chicago dance hall, I was paired with Mike Jameson. But not for a waltz. Mike used to earn a living as a bouncer, like so many fighters, and he hadn't started boxing until he was well into his twenties. But I figured he was better than his credentials suggested.

I was dead keen to impress my first American audience. Barry McGuigan and Lloyd Honeyghan, who were also on the trip, had won their fights on the undercard and were at ringside to cheer me on. They didn't have long to cheer. I jabbed Mike without anything coming back in the first round. He tried a bit in the second but the bouncer in him came out: he proved an easy target for a wicked left hook and a right uppercut. The combination put him out on his back. It was a good statement of my worth.

Angelo Dundee, one of the great names in boxing, reckoned I was the best young British heavyweight in a long time. This was some compliment coming from the man who trained Muhammad Ali. He said I should work on my mobility and develop slowly. The first piece of advice I couldn't argue with. But I was getting more and more tired of Terry's cautious strategy. And, when we returned to

London, it was back to the American tourists.

Bill Sharkey, a small heavyweight who had gone the distance with Weaver and drawn with LeDoux, should have been better opposition than he turned out to be. I knocked him out in a round.

But if I wanted someone to remind me of the dangers of professional boxing, he was waiting for me at the Albert Hall. His name was Floyd 'Jumbo' Cummings.

8

Growing Up with Harry

TO THIS DAY, I CAN FEEL THE PUNCH THAT JUMBO CUMMINGS HIT me with that Tuesday night in October 1983. I'd come a long way – eighteen months, eighteen wins and a rating in the top ten in the country – since I'd climbed into the ring with Lupe Guerra. Here I was again – the Albert Hall, end of the first round. Same place, different story. It looked like the whole show had ground to a halt.

I'd been winning the round easily, sticking my jab in Jumbo's face pretty much as I pleased. I had worked hard on my defence in the gym, and the counters he kept throwing weren't giving me any trouble.

Maybe I got cocky, maybe Jumbo wasn't the mug I thought he was, but I let him back me up on the ropes. I lined him up for a left hook to keep him at bay. It missed. Stupidly, I was standing there with my chin in the air and my mind obviously on something else – and he let go with a right. It was one of those nasty, looping punches, the ones you don't see. The ones that knock you out. I didn't know it at the time, but it was the special punch of another American heavyweight – 'Terrible' Tim Witherspoon. Jumbo had put most of his weight behind this one, and that was a lot of weight. When it arrived on the side of my jaw it probably had the power to bring down a small building.

This particular small building was nearly demolished. My eyes were looking in different directions; if it hadn't been for the ropes, I might have ended up in Hyde Park. I was gone. Somehow my legs kept me upright. And, luckily, there wasn't enough of the round left for Jumbo to finish me off.

I have to say I don't remember the fight as well as I'm describing it. The punch wiped out maybe half an hour of my life, and I've had to look at the tapes. But I have vague memories of the bell going and the referee Mike Jacobs guiding me towards the corner along the ropes. The look on Terry Lawless's face said it all. He must have been thinking, 'We're not in the Frank Bruno business any more.' I wasn't thinking anything.

I was in that world where there are no thoughts. It's hard to describe it unless you've been there. Muhammad Ali said once it was like falling through a trapdoor into a cellar full of crocodiles. It's an empty place with no sound, a lot of light. You see faces and watch people talking but you're not taking it in. You're floating. There isn't any pain because there's so much adrenalin running through your veins and your nervous system has been closed down by the force of the blow.

It was a comfort to see three familiar faces in the corner: Jimmy, Frank and Terry were there, as always. Jimmy and Frank had the smelling salts under my nose and were rubbing my neck and shoulders. I think they were shouting something in my ear too. I don't know how confident they were that I was back in the real world. Terry held up a couple of fingers and I told him, yes, there were two of them. 'Keep jabbing, Frank, keep jabbing,' he said. I nodded. I probably would have nodded if he'd asked me to run around the Albert Hall stark naked. I was out of it.

When the bell went for round two, they shoved me off my stool and I went back to work. I wasn't sure where I was or why I was supposed to be there. I just got on with what I had trained to do most of my life: fight. It's deep down in your brain. You do something often enough and it becomes second nature. It's like walking into your front room and turning the light switch on without looking. It's always there, in the same place. And my office, the ring, never changed. I sat on a stool, I moved out to the middle of the ring, I came back after three minutes. That was what I did when I went to work. Jimmy and Frank had put me through the routine day after day, week after week. I'd been doing the same thing for years, amateur and pro. Now I had to hope my instincts and my training would be enough to get me through.

Cummings had his blood up. He was one tough customer, a man with a colourful background, as they say. I'm not sure why he was called Jumbo but he was certainly a big boy. And he was lucky to be here. Sixteen years before, he'd shot a shop-keeper back in Mississippi. He was seventeen when he was banged up and he didn't get out until he was twenty-nine. When you've got that much time on your hands, there are plenty of things you can get up to. Jumbo learnt to box. The coaches at the Stateville Prison must have been pretty good because they say he knocked over George Foreman. But you're never sure what to believe in this game.

When Jumbo turned pro, he won fourteen straight. Renaldo Snipes, one of the best around at the time, was among his victims. Jumbo also fought an old Joe Frazier to a draw. His career had run out of steam a bit after that, but obviously he had a pedigree. You don't compete in that sort of company without being a decent fighter. And, on the evidence of his right hand, Jumbo Cummings was a decent fighter.

The trip to the States had given me confidence. Mixing it with the best had proved I'd gone up a level. I'd held my own with champions and guys who wanted to be champions, my combinations were getting sharper every day, my power was increasing with each fight. Physically I was better than ever: Frank had me in the shape of my life, my weight was steady at just under sixteen stone, I was free of injury. I thought I needed a real test, and this was the sort of opponent I wanted. It was the sort of opponent the critics wanted. Even Terry and Mickey had been keen – right up until Mr Cummings smacked me on the side of the head.

The second round was going to be the toughest of my career so far. Jumbo knew one good punch could put him back in the big time – he let me have it from all angles. I covered up and, in between bombs, I tried a jab or two. I was still getting my wits together. People see fighters looking in reasonable shape after taking a big punch and imagine they must be 100 per cent again. But it can take ages to get your brain unscrambled. Jumbo lined me up for the kill and got through with several heavy head shots. I survived.

Round two out of the way, and my corner was happy. They

reckoned I'd seen off the best Jumbo had to offer and, if I kept my boxing together, I'd win. I wasn't so sure that Jumbo was spent, having been on the business end of his best work for three minutes. But I understood what they were saying. Back in the land of the living – almost. The plan was to get in close and shorten my punches, to put a bit more dig in them and nail Jumbo properly as he got tired. He did.

I worked my way past his guard and made him suffer. My head was clearing slowly and I was able to concentrate on my boxing rather than worrying about Jumbo's. As he slowed down, he was easier to line up for the heavy shots. By the fifth he was getting desperate: he started butting me. I was so fired up about finishing him off, I ignored it. I had never been past five rounds, so the sixth was going to be an interesting learning experience. But I was strong, and Jumbo was getting weaker. He might not have been the best of trainers, because he was breathing like a beached whale. It was only a matter of time before he folded.

The end to my ordeal – and Jumbo's – came in the seventh. A right hook to the temple did for him and he went flying at a fair rate. He got up at seven but didn't look too clever. I was mightily relieved when the referee stepped in to call it off.

Looking back, beating Jumbo was the turning point I'd hoped for. I'd got more from the fight than just a headache. I knew now that I could take a really heavy shot. Up to that point only Joe Christle had hurt me, and that was back in the amateurs. After him, I'd pretty much been in control of every bout. Even after eighteen professional wins, I'd still felt like a novice. Now I could look in the mirror and call myself a pro. You never know how you'll handle a crisis until it arrives. It's a lesson I would learn for real years later – but it would take more than a sweet right hook to get out of Goodmayes. For the moment, I was just glad that I'd faced my first test and come through.

Nevertheless, the critics decided I must be chinny. One wobble and you're gone – that's all it takes for the instant experts to write you off. They want their heroes to be perfect. It makes for good headlines; it gives the fans a reason to believe in you, to believe you can become a world champion. It's a better story if you're unbeatable.

Sometimes I did wonder about a few of the press boys. If I thought they didn't know what they were talking about, I'd ask them: 'Are you a fighter or a writer?' What the first round of that fight proved was exactly the opposite of what they were saying. I'd taken an absolute nuclear bomb of a right hand. It would have floored nine out of ten heavyweights. In fact, it might have floored me but for the ropes. But somehow I got through the round – not to mention the punishment I took in the next. My instincts were strong, so was my conditioning and my heart. I fancied it. There was no question of quitting.

There are people who've never taken a punch on the whiskers who think they know what you're thinking, what's in your heart. I had bottle. If I was a quitter, if I was chinny, I had the best excuse in the world to give up in that first round. But I knew what I was made of. I knew what I wanted out of life. And what I knew was that I was in this business for real.

There was a lot to play for in 1983. Apart from Larry Holmes, the game didn't have any stand-out heavyweights.

It would be nearly two years before Mike Tyson came on the scene and, while he was learning his trade with Cus D'Amato, I was moving up the ratings.

There was a vacuum near the top of the division and a handful of fighters (including me) were desperate to fill it – Tim Witherspoon, Greg Page, Michael Dokes, Trevor Berbick, Lucien Rodriguez and Gerrie Coetzee. None of them had made much of an impact, either on the public or the legitimate champion. *The Ring* asked: 'Will Holmes's successor please stand up?' I fancied my chances against any of them, even then – although Terry wasn't so enthusiastic. It wasn't quite my time yet. It soon would be.

Boxing was in a bit of a mess. When isn't it? But the arrival of a new organising body, the International Boxing Federation, really stirred up the division. The WBA and the WBC reckoned the IBF were just trying it on. It didn't mean their first champion was a mug. In fact, it was Larry Holmes. He'd given up his WBC belt to become their title-holder, and no one could say he was slipping. Over at the WBC, Witherspoon was impressing a few people; he lost a split decision to Holmes in May. I thought he'd make for an interesting contest, but that would have to wait a while.

Terry and Mickey reckoned my best route to a title was with the WBA. They had more clout there, I think. The WBA's champion was Gerrie Coetzee, and he looked beatable. Just as importantly, it was a fight we thought we could bring to London. Coetzee was a white South African, and most contenders didn't want to get involved with him – especially in South Africa – because of the politics. People gave me stick for even considering the fight. As it turned out, it wouldn't happen then. Anyway, Greg Page got to him first – and knocked him out. I'd have to go a different route.

Boxing is not just a sport, it's showbiz. And the night I beat Jumbo I got into that side of the game, almost by accident. Funnily enough, I didn't recognise Harry Carpenter at first – then again I wasn't recognising too many people; it had been some punch . . .

The BBC had always sent Des Lynam to cover my fights before. Now here was this nice, smiling old guy in his suit and tie, with his glasses, neatly combed silver hair and a BBC voice, but not too posh. He looked more like a schoolteacher than someone who earned his living as a TV commentator at the fights. But I liked him straight away.

'That was some punch,' Harry said to me at ringside. 'You did well to recover from it.' I wasn't sure what he was talking about. This guy is having a bit of a laugh, I thought, so I played along. It gradually dawned on me he was talking about that Jumbo right hand. For the first time in an interview I dropped in a few 'know what I means', and, for some reason, it became my catchphrase. I can't tell you why. It's a common enough expression. I don't see what's so funny about it. But, say something often enough, and it becomes part of the culture. I suppose it didn't do any harm.

I was still making my name in boxing, but Harry was something of a legend. He knew the history of the game inside out and had been friends with most of the great fighters down the years. He'd been at ringside for some of the biggest fights in history. To me Harry's voice *was* boxing. One of my earliest boxing memories was Muhammad Ali beating George Foreman in the Rumble in the Jungle. I was thirteen at the time, but I still remember Harry coming out with: 'Oh my God, he's won the title back at thirty-two!' For a boxing guy like me, it was up there with 'They think it's all over . . .'

My Jumbo night wasn't quite Wembley '66. I'd just beaten an ex-con from Mississippi and I'd been lucky not to get knocked into the middle of the next week.

Over the years, Harry and I were very good for each other. We didn't set out to be a double act, but we reckoned it would be good for business to go with it. Harry was no fool. Neither was I. So we milked it. He would feed me fairly straight questions, knowing I'd give him a cheeky answer without going over the top. I think because I like to go near the knuckle it kept him on edge. He has a nice sense of humour and got a laugh out of my jokes. I was never sure if he understood them, mind you, but he laughed anyway. I hope people enjoyed it. It was innocent stuff.

Harry would become as much a part of my public life as Terry and Mickey. Bigger, probably – Harry was there in front of millions of viewers every fight. He was the guy with the microphone. Our partnership was very important to my career, because everyone picked up on it: the papers, the radio, TV – even *Spitting Image*. I didn't know then that image meant so much. I suppose it was the real start of the packaging of Frank Bruno. There was nothing I could do about it – and why should I?

In a couple of years' time, I wouldn't be able to go anywhere without being recognised. I liked performing. After four years in the business, it was no problem to mug for the cameras.

Having said that, it wasn't that much of an act. It came naturally to me, to laugh at life, to crack bad jokes, to be respectful to people. Some thought I was laying it on a bit thick, but anyone who knows me will tell you it's pretty much what I'm like. I'm not that good an actor. These days, I'm not so much in the limelight, so I don't have to keep up the performance. But I hope I'm essentially the same Frank I was when I was fighting for titles. In fact, the same Frank I was back in Barmouth Road. Yet the side I showed to the public was never the whole story. I was giving them what they wanted, not the real Frank.

After nineteen fights, my career was riding high. Any press conference Mickey called would get maximum coverage. I was pals with all the boxing writers – we knew each other pretty well by now, even the ones I didn't agree with – and it wasn't just the sports pages who were interested. I dressed up as Santa Claus, I kissed a few babies, I was there for the media whenever they wanted me. I had no problems with that. It went with the territory. I was even getting a lot of play in America – always a sign.

That Tuesday evening, as soon as I'd showered and changed at the Albert Hall, Laura and I headed off to Trattoria Parmigiana in the East End. Terry and his family were waiting. It was our favourite restaurant, and we'd celebrate many great nights there. The whole place stood up and cheered when we walked in. It was a very moving moment. I felt at home. Some days, I wish it could have been like that for ever, Laura and I going back to Trattoria Parmigiana and meeting up with Terry and Sylvia and all the others. Life was uncomplicated. We were all one big family. For now, the world was ours. The BBC were happy, my manager and promoter were happy, and Laura, Nicola and I were happy. How could it ever go wrong?

Now there was a new page written into my story. After Jumbo, there was the excitement factor. There was the chance that the whole show might end in one punch. We hadn't planned it that way, but there was no getting away from it – people weren't sure if I would go over from a big right hand. It would stay with me for the rest of my career.

It took me weeks to read all the letters I got. People said I showed real grit to get through that first round, then come back to finish it off. Not long before, the same fans had booed as I put away yet another tourist. I went back to the gym and concentrated on my job.

Within two months I was back in the ring, at the Albert Hall again. I really liked the place. It's probably the most perfect space there is to watch boxing, a huge circle with boxes above. There have been so many memorable fights in the Albert Hall, going back to the twenties. Sometimes, though, the opposition don't live up to the surroundings, and my next opponent, Walter 'Mad Dog' Santemore, wasn't too special.

Santemore was another big American – six five and just over sixteen stone – although not a big puncher. He was thirty-two, an ex-cop from New Orleans, and he'd been in with – and lost to – some decent fighters, including Bonecrusher Smith and my old mates Quick Tillis and Jeff Sims. Walter wasn't expected to cause me much trouble. He didn't. A fighter they told me was a cagey operator turned out to be a bit of a clown. He even tried an Ali shuffle. I cut him under the left eye in the first round, then went to work on the rest of him for another three rounds before I put a huge right on his chin and we all said goodnight.

I rested up over Christmas before getting ready for my next fight, at Wembley in March. Terry and Mickey had got me a right beanpole, a thirty-year-old Argentine called Juan Figueroa. He didn't have much of a record. Maybe he'd been picked for his nickname, because it was the best yet I'd come across: 'The Giant of the Market'. He was called that, if you were wondering, because he was six foot six and worked in a market. Juan lasted sixty-seven seconds.

I was embarrassed. Not for the first time. But after Jumbo I thought I'd done with the walkovers. I thought I would be moving on a bit. What was the point of fighting giant gardeners from Argentina and ex-cops from New Orleans? So far, Terry's strategy had panned out perfectly, but I wasn't sure too many more of these fights would be good for my career.

If I wasn't burning up much energy at the Albert Hall, I was training harder than ever at the Royal Oak. I loved it. For a big man, I do a lot of running. If you haven't got the miles on the clock you'll find out pretty soon: in the fifth or sixth round of a fight, maybe. That's when you need your wind. If you've cheated on your training, you'll be found out. You can spot fighters who haven't done their stamina work because they start to get a bit nervous as the rounds go by; they take longer rests, move out of range for a breather and don't put as much into their punches. Then their concentration goes and they're there for the taking. I was determined not to make that mistake. It proved to be harder than I thought.

Nobody wins for ever, although I sometimes thought I would. Jumbo Cummings had given me a scare and I came through. If anything, it made me more certain I was going to make it. Then I met a man called James 'Bonecrusher' Smith.

I was just about finished with the Bum of the Month Club. Now that I was on the rise and dangerous there would be bigger gaps between fights. That was because opponents wanted more money to get in the ring with me, and those sort of negotiations took a little longer. I had two months to get ready for James Smith.

Bonecrusher was a funny, fast-talking American, like so many of them in the boxing business. He was a former GI with a big right hand. He reckoned he could crush your bones with a single punch, and his nickname was more threatening than the 'Giant of the Market'. I've certainly never forgotten it.

Although Bonecrusher started his boxing career late, he was considered one of the most dangerous men in the division. He'd put together thirteen wins in a row and was on a roll. But that was my job, looking for danger. You didn't get to the top fighting fat guys from nowhere. This was a contest I really wanted. I knew I was up to it and I wanted to show the world.

'Frank, once you've got Bonecrusher out the way, Mike Weaver's next,' Terry told me. This was what we'd been working towards. Weaver was a former champ, and Terry reckoned he'd got us a date for September. Beating Weaver

would put me right in the spotlight in America. More importantly, it would leave me only a couple of fights away from a
title shot. I could almost taste it, I was that close.

It turned out to be a strange night, that 13 May at the
Wembley Arena. My gym-mate, Mark Kaylor, was on the under-
card. Like me, Mark was a fighter on the way up. He was a
middleweight and in cracking form – so good, in fact, that
Terry and Mickey took a bit of a chance with his opponent.
The guy they brought over for him, Buster Drayton, was on
the small side – he was really a light middleweight – but he
could bang. And bang he did. He knocked Mark down five
times then stopped him in the seventh. Mark took a serious
hiding. We could hardly believe it – although looking back
it should have been a warning. One punch can be enough,
any time from any fighter. Mark was devastated. We tried to
put it out of our minds but it was hard. There was an awful
mood in the dressing room when I gloved up to go and meet
the Bonecrusher.

Funny thing about the Wembley Arena. If they sold all
the seats, there'd be as big a crowd as the Albert Hall. If
they didn't sell out, they'd bring in a big black curtain to
make the place seem smaller. It gave it atmosphere. On
some lesser fights, that black curtain would get pretty close
to the ring. Not tonight. It was a full house and the place
was buzzing. They expected a big performance from me, a
get-square for Mark.

Smith was an unusual fighter. He would later become the
first heavyweight champion of the world to own a university
degree. Not sure it's necessary to be an intellectual to fight,
although Chris Eubank may tell you different. Apparently,

Bonecrusher had originally only turned pro for pocket money. And here he was, about twenty feet across the ring from me, eyes and muscles bulging.

As Terry had told me, there was a lot riding on this fight. NBC were showing it coast to coast in the States. The word had been spreading in the industry about my knockout record and the Americans wanted to see for themselves what all the noise was about. I looked over at Bonecrusher and saw more than an opponent. I saw someone blocking my way to the world title. I could almost see that belt around my waist.

I'd come in at a bit under sixteen stone, about six pounds lighter than Smith. He was an inch taller too. But those are just figures. At our weight, it's how comfortable you feel that matters. I was still growing; later, I'd be just as happy fighting at nearly a stone heavier. Now, though, I was an up-and-coming 23-year-old, desperate to make my mark. We were only three years into my career, and it looked like I was well on track.

I started the fight well. It wasn't one of my most devastating performances, there were no explosions. But I was happy enough with my boxing: the jab was working well and Bonecrusher rarely got within breathing distance of my ribs. At the weigh-in he'd threatened he'd be all over me but, frankly, it wasn't that sort of fight. Bonecrusher had his ambitions too, of course. He wanted to be in the big picture back in the States. Maybe he was conscious of not looking bad. That can happen. You become too aware of the cameras sometimes and you lose your rhythm. It wasn't a problem for me, because I'd been in the spotlight nearly my whole career. But this night I was more workmanlike than exciting.

Bonecrusher's right eye was bruising up nicely by the end of the eighth round. I was cruising to a comfortable points win. Two rounds left. 'Just keep it up, Frank,' Terry said at the end of the ninth. 'Three more minutes and then we can all go back to the Parmigiana.'

If only I'd listened. I'm still not sure what went wrong. I'd won every round; I only had to hold Bonecrusher off with my jab and it would be twenty-two wins from twenty-two fights, with bigger and better things to come. Maybe my ego got the better of me. I was so confident I decided I'd knock him out. A nice right cross, bang on the chin – that would get the guys at NBC out of their seats.

Well, I threw the right. And it missed. Bonecrusher's left hook didn't. It landed square on the side of my jaw. All of a sudden I had the ropes for company. As with Jumbo's right hand, I wasn't sure how it had happened. I don't remember seeing it. It's always the way when you get hurt. If you see the punch coming, you instinctively make arrangements. You either sway away from it, or stick a glove in the way. I did neither.

There were more to follow. Unlike Jumbo, Bonecrusher had time to go to work. His eyes were nearly popping out of their sockets as he thrashed away. They counted fourteen unanswered haymakers. Don't ask me. I was too busy stopping them. With my face. Until I sank to the floor.

When the count started, I grabbed on to the ropes and tried to haul myself up. I knew it was near the end of the fight – if I could just get through it, I would win. All my instincts told me to get up, but it was funny: I couldn't make my legs work. I tried again. Then again. They were having none of it. I was counted out for the only time in my life. It was as if my world had come to an end. I can't tell you how horrible it felt.

'The Bruno bubble is burst!' Harry Carpenter shouted to his viewers. He reckoned it was over. So did a lot of people. Terry looked down into the press seats at Harry Mullan, the editor of the trade paper, the *Boxing News*. Harry hadn't been convinced about me. 'Suppose you're happy now,' Terry said. Harry said nothing.

Jimmy, Frank and Terry rushed over and picked me up, guiding me back to the corner, the same corner they had taken Mark Kaylor to about an hour before. Sydney Hulls, a veteran boxing writer whose family had been in the game for generations, wrote in the *Daily Express* that it was 'our greatest double fighting disaster in years'. The night had a really bad feel about it, from start to finish.

And it got worse. Terry was devastated. I'd never seen him like this before. I'm not sure if he cried but he was entitled to. Laura was crushed too. Oddly, once we were back in the dressing room, I was probably the least upset. Certainly it was a setback and I would wake up with a decent headache. But I tried to put it in perspective. Worse things happen at sea, as they say. None of that washed with Terry.

'I think that's it for me, Frank,' he said. 'I'm not sure I can carry on in this game. I don't know what you want to do but, if you decide to keep boxing, maybe you should get yourself another manager. I'm going to pack it in.'

I didn't know what to say. This was the man who'd told

me it would be a long, hard slog to the top, that we wouldn't do it overnight and that there'd be times when we might feel like giving up. Now he was going to walk away. Maybe he was right. Maybe I should quit too. I wasn't sure I wanted to carry on without Terry. We'd been through so much together, it wouldn't be the same with someone else.

Laura and I went home, and talked long and hard about it. The next morning, my head still throbbing, I sat down at the kitchen table and stared into my orange juice. I had a big decision to make and I didn't want to rush into it. I had come into this business to better myself, because the alternatives were dire. Was it all over? Was I not really good enough?

All that morning I thought about the fight and my future. I'd earned decent money but nowhere near the sums that had been just a couple of fights away. And those couple of fights could have made me a world champion. That did it for me. How could I get so close to achieving what I'd set out to and then just give up after one defeat? The day I fought Bonecrusher would have been Joe Louis' seventieth birthday. Joe had always been an inspiration to me: he lost and he got up. So would I. Like Ali did. Like all the great champions. I'm not saying I was in their class, but I knew I hadn't been the best I could be yet. Not by a long way. There was a lot left. I picked up the phone and rang Terry at his home in Essex. He was asleep and didn't want to know. But Sylvia insisted.

'Terry, don't give up now,' I said. 'We're too close. I can still make it. I know I can. It was a bad night, that's all. It's not as if I was at the end of my career. I'm at the start. You said it would take five or six years. Let's keep going.'

And we did. We walked into the post-fight press conference

together. Terry told it like it was: it had been a huge setback, but it wasn't the end. We were still going to make it. It would just take a little longer.

I knew why Terry was so upset. We were close and I was his friend as well as his fighter. But it was a money thing too. He and Mickey had invested a lot of dough in me. Now, so close to a big title shot, I'd been knocked out. It was as if I'd let him down. But I didn't think I had. I had boxed well enough right up to the last round. That's when my lack of experience showed. I ignored the corner's orders, certainly, but I wasn't brutally beaten up. I hadn't been belted for ten whole rounds. It was short and not so sweet – and I still had the hunger.

More than any easy win, defeat made me stronger. I was now desperate for the world title. However long it took, nothing was going to stop me.

9

Redemption, Bruises and Lawyers

BOXING'S ABOUT PAIN. EVERY DAY – WHETHER YOU'RE RUNNING ten miles on the road or doing your floor exercises, bashing away at the heavy bag or going five rounds in sparring – you're working your body as hard as you can. And it's all for that half-hour in the ring. You can like your opponent, you can know it's just business, you can duck and weave and slip punches like you're a magician, but in the end it's about hurting the other guy. Enough to make him stop.

A lot of boxers don't know when to call it a day. They get badly hurt – they end up brain-damaged. Punch-drunk. Getting hit in the head is what you sign up for. But one good punch can do it. Especially in the heavyweights.

I've been lucky. I never took what I'd call a serious hiding, and, touch wood, there have been no lasting effects. But it took me a while to recover from my encounter with Bonecrusher. It wasn't the pain or any injury. It was the hangover from the experience. Everything came crashing down that night. I'd been climbing through the division, an unbeaten prospect with everyone's hopes to carry with me. Physically, I was fine. But I was down mentally.

There was never really any question that I'd quit, though. If you're going to be a fighter you can't worry about getting hurt or badly beaten about – otherwise you'd never get in the ring.

The people it got to were those who loved me. I don't think Laura ever enjoyed me boxing much, though she'd never have told me. She was really supportive – always – and she wanted me to do what I felt was right. She knew I could make a go of it, even after I'd lost. If she said a prayer every time I stepped into the ring, she knew me well enough to hide it.

My mother was another story. Not long before, she'd given an interview to *All Sport* magazine that shocked me. 'I hate the sport,' she said, 'but I wouldn't stop Frank because a man has to find his own way in life.' I hadn't realised how deeply she felt about it. I hadn't realised how worried she got.

Mum is a wonderful woman, the rock of our family. Until recently she was preaching at the Pentecostal church in Fulham and, trust me, she is inspirational – she's one powerful, powerful preacher. And she tried to bring us up the right way. It can't have been easy. In the same interview she told the journalist: 'Franklin believes in the Lord but he's still a sinner. He asks for His protection but he refuses to obey His commandments.' That was a bit of a dig at Laura and me: at the time we were living together but we weren't married. And we had a baby. It didn't sit well with my mother's beliefs. But she knew deep down that I was a good son. It was the boxing that really gave her a problem.

I suppose I'd always known she thought getting punched in the head for a living wasn't too smart. Now, though, she'd told me – and all the world – that she truly loathed it. I think the only reason she tolerated me fighting was because it was better than getting into trouble or labouring for a living. But I'd just taken what looked like a hell of a beating. I didn't know what she was going to say. The last thing I wanted to do was upset her.

I should have read that article more carefully: she meant what she said about my boxing, both bits of it. Yes, she hated the sport, but it was my life, and I had to make my own way. I've always been grateful to her.

The board won't even let you set foot in the gym for twenty-eight days after a stoppage defeat. I spent those four weeks plotting my future with Terry. Weaver was off the menu for the moment, and it was time to start again. I'd work out my frustrations on some lesser opponents and then convince Terry I was ready to go back in with the big boys.

As soon as those twenty-eight days were up, I was back in the gym. Training has always been the focus of my day and, because of what happened to me a couple of years ago when I gave it up for a while, I cherish it. Look after your body and your soul will feel good too. I always trained to near the limit, pushing myself all the way. And now that I'd lost, I was going to try even harder. It was good to get physical again, to feel the pain of the workout. But pretty soon I was wearing myself into the ground.

It was Frank Black who first noticed. 'Don't overdo it, Frank,' he told me. I didn't listen. I was young and strong and saw no need to hold back. I stepped up my roadwork – I was doing fifty miles every week, sometimes more – and I'd have been in the gym all night if someone had paid the electrics. My abs were as hard as a brick wall. I looked awesome.

How wrong could I be. You don't win titles by having the best abs. All this work was doing me more harm than good and I didn't realise it. I soon woke up, though. Because Frank insisted. I scaled back on the real energy-sapping stuff and learnt to keep the engine ticking over at a steady rate, rather than revving it up and braking hard.

That year Gary Mason joined us at the Royal Oak. He was a talented fighter and an obvious rival. Gary's a funny guy. He worked as a jeweller and opened a shop called Punch and Jewellery. But he didn't like training as much as I did. I think Terry was frustrated with him because he had so much natural talent. He had quick hands and moved well, even if he did carry a bit extra most of his career. I always thought if he'd put in a little more effort, he might have gone further in the game. As it was, he had to retire with an eye injury after his last fight, against Lennox Lewis in 1994. I still see Gary now and again. And he's still a joker.

We gave each other some excellent workouts, without ever trying to knock the bark off. The big guys can't afford to unload too much in the gym against fighters from the same stable. It's just too much of a risk. For serious sparring, Terry used to bring over guys from the States. I gave them hell. It sounds cruel to those outside the business, but it's just work to us. That's what they get paid for. Joe Louis, I'm told, used to knock out his best friend all the time when they sparred.

A few rounds with the hired hands soon got my confidence back up, and I was feeling good again. I'd put the Bonecrusher defeat behind me, I thought. But there's always a doubt until there's something on the line. I wouldn't know if things were really back on track until I got back in the ring. And that's where Terry came in. I kept asking him to get me a fight. He must have got sick of it.

One Monday morning I walked into the gym and made straight for Terry, as normal. Before he'd even had a chance to say hello I asked him the usual question: 'Who's next?' He seemed distracted, and it wasn't just because he was tired of me going on at him. Terry was staring at a copy of the *Sunday Times*. It wasn't happy reading. The paper had got hold of some documents that suggested Terry, Mickey, Jarvis Astaire and Mike Barrett had a loose business arrangement. I knew they were close, so I wondered what the fuss was about – it's how I thought the boxing business worked.

According to the article, the problem was this: Terry was negotiating with his partners while managing me. That was a conflict of interest, it claimed. Terry and I were partners, he'd always said. I didn't fancy going through the accounts, though. I was happy to leave the business side of things to him. All I knew was my career was in good hands. We may not have always agreed, but nothing in life is perfect.

The article caused a bit of a stir, and the board launched an investigation. We were all behind Terry on this one. 'As far as I'm concerned, Terry is the best manager in the world,' I told the papers. Three months later, the board cleared 'the Cartel', as the papers were calling Terry, Mickey and the boys. I was relieved that things were back to normal. No more suits getting in the way. I just wanted a fight – I'd been out for four months, the longest spell of my career so far. Someone was going to pay.

My comeback fight – because that's the way it always feels after a defeat – was against a pretty good Canadian called Ken Lakusta. It was back to the scene of the crime, too: Wembley Arena. If this didn't get rid of the demons, nothing would. I was yet to win any sort of title and this was an eliminator for the Commonwealth championship. It gave the fight an extra edge – although, because of the way my career went later, I never did fight for that belt.

I was on fire. For the four and a half minutes the fight lasted, Lakusta was on the receiving end of a bit of a pasting. I got rid of my frustrations the way I always have, letting the punches go. Lakusta wasn't a no-hoper. He was twenty-nine and had a decent record. But there was no way he could live with me that night. The previous year, he'd been ten rounds with Trevor Berbick, who would go on to take a slice of the world title – and he reckoned I hit a lot harder. I believe him. When I caught him on the side of the head, his legs went to jelly. He was hanging on to me like I was his mother. And I wasn't his mother, I can tell you. I was his daddy.

I'd shown the world I was back in business, and I made Lakusta suffer. I don't take pleasure in that: it's what you have to do. You can't afford to be half-hearted in boxing. You have to separate your work from your emotions. You have to be cold and professional. Otherwise, opponents will pick up on any doubts you might have. It's a mind game, as much as anything else.

I'm not really someone who's drawn to violence. In fact, since I learnt to control my temper at Oak Hall, I've always walked away from confrontation. A few years ago, someone had a go at me outside Wembley after a football match and he really got under my skin. Luckily for him (and me, I guess), someone got between us. I'd have been in big trouble with the board – and probably the law – if I'd got into a brawl outside the ring.

I don't need to prove anything, which is what a lot of street fights are about. Guys get worked up, or drunk, and have to show the world how tough they are. It's a bit sad – especially because most of them are useless at it. Unfortunately, my next fight wasn't much better than a pub row. I'd have been better off picking my opponent from the drunks on Wandsworth High Street on a Saturday night.

'I want to keep busy,' I'd told Terry.

'Fine, Frank. How about six weeks' time at the Albert Hall?'

It wasn't the biggest build-up I'd ever had. And the contest more than lived down to its billing – I can't imagine the Albert Hall has seen many worse. Jeff Jordan said he'd won seventeen of his twenty fights. I hate to think what the guys he beat were like.

I don't think our Jeffrey threw a proper punch in three rounds. By that time, I'd had enough. I'd cut him over the left eye and belted him all around the ring before the referee called the travesty off. It was one of those nights when I couldn't get out of the hall fast enough. I wanted fights, not total mismatches like this one.

Just three weeks later I was back at the Wembley Arena. It was one of the shortest rests I ever had between fights. But then the Jordan fixture wasn't exactly a fight. As far as I was concerned, I'd had tougher workouts against the heavy bag.

Now, though, I had a decent opponent, Phil Brown, an ex-con from New Orleans. It wasn't compulsory to have a criminal record to get a fight with me – but it seemed to help. Going by his record, Brown had every right to be here. Not long before, he'd managed to go twenty-two fights unbeaten. Many years later he would give Lennox Lewis a good fight for his world title. But this was 1984, and he was coming to me on the back of a fourth-round knockout at the hands of Gerry Cooney.

Despite what they say, the stats can lie. Brown turned out to be another runner; all he wanted to do was survive. It was so frustrating. I was back in prime shape and I really wanted to nail him. I can't think of another fight when I was so mucked about. He knew every trick in the book. He hugged me like a brother, then pushed me away as if I was asking him for money. Every time I got a couple of good digs in he managed to wriggle away. I won every round, so all his running achieved was to wind me up and get the boo-boys going in the crowd. But I'd been taken the distance for the first time in my career.

It wasn't the best of nights, and I can't say I was too pleased by my performance, especially when I read what the papers had to say. Joe Frazier was quoted as saying I 'boxed like a robot'. Joe was a great fighter, but I think he was a bit out of order making that call. It was the first time he'd seen me fight – and it's hard to look your best when you're up against someone who isn't interested. Still, it's nice to be noticed, and maybe he had a point. I knew I had to work on my movement.

I thought I'd left fights like these behind me. It was more than a year since I'd fought Jumbo, and that was supposed to be the turning point. The Phil Browns of this world weren't going to get my career moving again. I needed to pick up the pace again after the shock of Bonecrusher.

Terry kept telling me to keep the faith. I'd hear it over and over again. In twenty-five fights, I'd had one bad loss, and knocked over some pretty ordinary opponents. Now was the time to start thinking about titles. That would give me credibility in the trade. The Lonsdale Belt wasn't right for business reasons, even though it had a lot of prestige, and the Commonwealth championship wasn't going to happen either. The only other title to go for at this stage was the European. Terry told me to rest over Christmas. He'd see what he could do.

On 26 March 1985 I was on my way to the Wembley Arena again. I'd boxed there so often I felt like I owned the place. My opponent, the Frenchman Lucien Rodriguez, threatened to be a decent test, given his record. Not long before, he'd gone in against Larry Holmes and put up a fair show, losing on points. But that wasn't why we wanted him. If I beat Rodriguez – and I had no doubts I would – I would be in line for a shot at Anders Eklund, the European champion. I really wanted the Swede's title, so this was a fight with no room for error. This time I wasn't going to pull any stunts of the Bonecrusher variety – like looking for a last-round knockout. 'Get him out of there early if you can, Frank,' was the only thing Terry said.

If Brown was just a runner, Rodriguez was trickier. But

he didn't get much of a chance to show off his sprinting skills. He was a stone lighter than me, and when he felt my stiff left jab, I could see 'the look' in his eyes. You can't miss it. It's a mixture of fear and amazement. I could tell straight away he didn't fancy it. It felt pretty good: I was facing down a man who had gone the distance with the world champion only two years before. By the time I had backed him on to the ropes, Rodriguez was there for the taking – and we were still only in the first round. A right uppercut and a right hook did the job. He staggered up and just beat the count, but he looked like he wanted to be somewhere else. The referee agreed. Rodriguez shook his head and walked back to his corner. Fight over.

It was a good night's work. Especially as Anders Eklund was in the audience. Terry had got his man. Our title fight was only a month away and Eklund had come to check out what he was up against. I don't think he was thrilled at the prospect. I was delighted: I had my first title shot. But a fight is never on until the bell goes.

Just as we were getting down to work again at the Royal Oak, who should turn up but Burt McCarthy. I'd almost forgotten about our Burt, but there was no way he'd forgotten about me. It was rotten timing. Six months of legal wrangling followed and it really messed up my preparations. To make matters worse, we had lawyers coming at us from all sides.

Mickey and Mike Barrett had put up £200,000 to win the purse bid for the Eklund fight. I was getting £80,000 – maybe it's not a lot by the standards of world title fights, but I thought it was serious enough corn. Given that Anders was getting £120,000 I reckoned he should be pleased. But his manager, Mogens Palle, wasn't happy with his share of the TV rights and it all kicked off. Mickey went in hard against him. He was not a man to argue with lightly, over anything. It took so long to sort out, the fight was postponed until 1 October.

I liked Anders, who was a quietly spoken and respectful man, not like some of the loud Americans I'd seen off over the years. But I wasn't in the mood for pleasantries. As incredible as it seems, I'd been in the High Court the morning of the fight, watching Terry settle with Burt. I think it cost £60,000 all told, but there were a lot of big figures flying around at the time. If I needed any motivation, I had it now. It would take a few more pay days like this one to make up for that little mistake.

Anders was a big man, six foot six and probably a stone and a half heavier than me, so he wasn't the daintiest of movers. But it didn't take long to work out he was no mug. Towards the end of the first round he rocked me with a couple of heavy rights to the head. After that, it was a different story. I hurt him in the second and again in the third. He was just hanging in there, throwing nothing back. I knew I had him then. It was all over early in the fourth: I caught him with a right uppercut and two heavy head shots that pitched him flat on his face.

At last I had a title. It gave me such a lift. I'd proved I was up to the task in good company; I'd put my setbacks behind me and I'd made the critics eat their words. I just wished Joe Frazier could have been there to see me. It might be a little late to send him a tape.

As it turned out, a Frazier was my next opponent – a 36-year-old American called Larry 'Bad Boy' Frazier. He'd just got out of Soledad Maximum Security Center in California, having served two years for assaulting a police officer. At times I wondered if I was going to take on the entire prison population of the United States. Bad Boy stepped in at the last minute as a substitute for another Larry, Alexander, which wasn't ideal. Bad Boy – or Late Larry as I like to think of him – had lost two out of three fights since his release, but he had been a better fighter than that. I'd soon find out if he had any of the old juice that saw him once knock out the former world champion Mike Weaver – as well as my mate Jeff Sims.

I needn't have worried too much about Late Larry. He went down and out in the second on my return to the Albert Hall three weeks before Christmas. 'I've never been hit so hard,' he told reporters.

I made another hit at the end of '85, playing Juliet to Lenny Henry's Romeo, at the Shaftesbury Theatre for Comic Relief. It was my first acting stint. I bet Judi Dench was quaking in her boots.

Now for 1986 – the year my brother had predicted I would be world champion back on the kitchen wall in Barmouth Road. Things had been going so well since Bonecrusher I thought I had a good chance of making his words come true. But Terry wasn't buying Michael's Mystic Meg act. He didn't think I was ready to go for it just yet. 'You're still learning, Frank,' he said. 'There's plenty of time. And you don't want to be fighting for the title for peanuts. We want to get as much money as we can. Leave it to Mickey and me. We haven't done too badly so far.'

I knew I needed to fine-tune a few things, but I was nearly there. I'd worked extra hard on my defence, boxing with my gloves up around my chin a bit more. Jimmy and Frank were happy with my improvement – but what really pleased them was my power. Amazingly, I was still getting stronger. It felt so good when the big punches connected – it was as if I could knock out an elephant. I told Terry and Mickey that I was running out of patience. I didn't want any more Late Larrys, no more fall guys with long rap sheets and short attention spans. Mickey wasn't quite as cautious as Terry. Off he went to the States to see what he could do.

In September 1985 Larry Holmes's long reign as the recognised champion had come to an end at the hands of Michael Spinks. Now that Holmes was gone, the heavyweight division really was in a mess. At the centre of the chaos – as usual – was Don King.

Don was some item. He could sell you your own teeth. I admired him in some ways, because he came up from the streets and made the most of what he got. He might not have always done things by the book, and there were plenty of people who had good reason to hate the sight of him, but, if you wanted a big fight, you nearly always had to go through Don. And he knew it. He pretty much had the heavyweights tied up.

King told the world he was trying to unify the titles. It usually suited Don if the WBC, WBA and IBF kept their belts separate. Three titles meant three times as much money. Mickey had a plan to break into Don's game. The mandatory challenger for the WBA version was the South African Gerrie Coetzee. Because of the political situation in South Africa,

Mickey gambled on bringing him to London to fight me – which wasn't quite as bad as having to go to the home of apartheid. If I beat Coetzee I would take his place as mandatory challenger. And King would be hard-pressed to keep me out of the picture then.

Mickey was right when he said there would be aggravation over Coetzee. Some people, including my mates John Conteh and Maurice Hope, told me not to take the fight – they were worried Coetzee would be held up as some sort of champion of apartheid. I'm sure Gerrie wasn't racist, though. And I didn't think pulling out of the fight would help the black population of South Africa. I know people disagreed with me – some of them have never forgiven me. I respect their point of view. It wasn't as if I didn't care about my black brothers. Of course I did. But at the time, I didn't see how it would make any difference.

Whatever the wrongs and rights of it, the fight was on – at Wembley Arena – and I was determined to show the world I was worthy of a world title shot.

Coetzee had lost only four times in thirty-four contests, though two of those losses had been in his last two fights. Still, he had a right hand nearly as lethal as mine, so I'd have to get in early to stop him using it. It was a simple plan, and I was sure it would work as soon as he took his robe off. There was only one word to describe him: fat. It didn't look like he'd put the work in for this one. Maybe he thought it would be an easy night. It was. For me.

I started fast and finished early. My jab bamboozled Coetzee. He didn't know what to do, except move backwards – in straight lines. And that goes against all the coaching advice. If you're going to move back, move back and to the side. If you go in a straight line you're not very hard to find. And find Gerrie is what I did. I had him down midway through the first round with probably as sweet a right as I have ever thrown. It was a long one, like a rocket, and when it exploded Gerrie must have thought he was back in his bed in South Africa. I almost felt sorry for him. It was all over, just one minute and twenty seconds after we'd started. That's what I call a good night's work. A few judges thought I wasn't up to it. It was a great feeling to prove them wrong. I've been doing it all my life.

I'd delivered my part of the deal; now it was up to Mickey and Terry to do the business with Don King. In my book, the odds on it going smoothly were extremely long. I was right.

10

Terrible Tim, Terrible Night

'FRANK, I'VE GOT SOME GREAT NEWS,' TERRY TOLD ME A COUPLE OF months after I'd knocked out Gerrie Coetzee. 'It looks like we can get Witherspoon to fight you in London later this year.'

'Terrible' Tim Witherspoon was the WBA heavyweight champion. Beating Coetzee had made me the mandatory challenger, but you learn to take nothing for granted in boxing. Mickey's good work, the endless negotiations with Don King, had paid off.

'You're not serious,' was all I could say. It was hard to take it in – we'd been working towards this day for six years. It was going to be the biggest fight the country had ever seen – bigger even than Henry Cooper against Muhammad Ali twenty years earlier. Life was looking good. Our second child, Rachel, had arrived and I was earning serious money. I'd left the building sites far behind me. 'Frank Bruno: Heavyweight Champion of the World.' It had a nice ring to it – but I always tried to keep my feet on the ground.

The experts didn't think much of Witherspoon, and they regarded his WBA title as inferior to the WBC belt. When I watched the tapes, I thought Witherspoon was underrated. The WBA title wasn't the biggest prize, but it was easy to see he was a good champion. Maybe he didn't look the part – he wasn't exactly slimline – but he was a skilful fighter, with a dangerous overarm right. Not many boxers throw that one. When it connects it usually comes down near the temple, which is the place to aim for if you want to send an opponent wobbling like a ninepin. It happened to me against Jumbo Cummings, and it's worse than getting tagged on the chin, believe me.

It's just as well I didn't get too carried away. Before I could get Witherspoon in the ring he failed a drugs test – for marijuana, ironically enough, my chosen method of relaxing after a fight. If Terry and Mickey had found out I was doing a bit of puff, there'd have been murders. Somehow – I didn't trouble myself with the details of these sort of things – Witherspoon was allowed to hang on to his title. The fight was still on. We were due to meet on 19 July, but a lot could happen between now and then.

I knew I'd arrived in the big time when they told me we'd be fighting at Wembley Stadium. To get the American money, we had to go out live on HBO, the big pay-per-view channel over there. That meant the fight couldn't start till one in the morning. For the public, it was a shame it wasn't being shown live here. But at least more of my fans got to see me at the bigger venue – and, of course, we took more money at the gate.

There was an almighty row between the BBC and ITV over

the UK rights. The BBC had televised all my fights, but ITV were desperate for this one. In the end it was settled by the toss of a coin, believe it or not. ITV got to screen the fight first, at nine thirty the following morning. The BBC showed it on Sunday night.

Things went a little bit crazy. The whole country was behind me. The papers went overboard. And I worried about the postman's back, I was getting so many letters. 'You can do it, Frank,' was the sort of thing people wrote. 'Bring us home the title.' They were desperate to have a British world heavyweight champion. I felt a huge responsibility to do it for them – like Tim Henman must experience every Wimbledon. Our football team get the same treatment every World Cup. Unless you've been through it, you can't understand the pressure. I could only hope it didn't all get to me on the night of the fight.

There was no doubt it was going to be more than just another big fight. Boxing was my job and my life, but I had become an entertainer too. This was big-time showbiz; it was like being a rock star. Almost exactly a year before, people had filled the same stadium for Live Aid. Now everyone wanted a ticket for my fight.

Whatever his faults, Don King was in his element. Nobody cracks worse jokes. Nobody draws up weirder contracts. Nobody sells more tickets. He's so full of tricks, you're never sure what's going to happen next – which is why he pulls in the crowds. This is the man who, for a couple of months, took over an entire African country to stage the Rumble in the Jungle. He even persuaded the hero of that fight to come to London to drum up business. It was sad, in a way. Ali had retired five years earlier and, even then, it was obvious he was on the long way down.

Ali was the fighter I loved more than any other. I'd met him when I was a teenage prospect. 'Get up on your toes and dance, Frank,' he told me then. As if. But I had the utmost respect for the man. Which is more than I can say for Terrible Tim's people.

When Witherspoon finally made it over from the States, I thought he'd brought the whole country with him. It was the first time I'd run up against a real boxing posse. A lot of the guys I'd been fighting had come on their own, or maybe with their trainer. Witherspoon's people crashed in with their flash jackets and shades, like some sort of street gang. They made a hell of a racket.

I kept my head down and did my best to ignore them. I was so focused during the build-up, everyone thought I'd turned into a hermit. It was a pretty simple routine: get up, go to the gym, come home, go to bed. It can't have been easy on my family, but I had to be at my very best for this one, and I really didn't want any distractions. Terry agreed.

The press weren't so keen, especially when I barred them from my training sessions. They said I was panicking, that I couldn't handle the pressure. In fact, I've never liked people watching me train. Years later, I even threw one sneaky *Observer* journalist out of a gym myself. But I'd given them all they'd wanted for six years. Now it was time for them to give me some space. I needed every edge I could get. If Witherspoon hadn't trained properly, I wanted to be in the best possible condition to take advantage.

Witherspoon may have travelled with a bunch of loud-mouths, but he was a professional. I didn't really expect him to turn up underdone. So when he refused to show the boxing writers what sort of shape he was in, I was a bit surprised. When he eventually took his top off, I was as shocked as they were. He didn't look like he'd run twenty yards in training. I'd done hundreds of miles and so I felt even more confident now. What I didn't realise was that was how Tim looked all the time. He had a smooth, round shape rather than a muscled-up one. I was about to find out there was nothing wrong with his stamina.

'This is what we're in business for,' Terry said, as we gloved up in the dressing room. 'You've earned it, now go out there and give it everything. You might never get another chance.'

I was absolutely buzzing. I was so strong and determined, I didn't for a second think I could lose. I was convinced the title was mine. So were the 40,000 fans who'd turned up to cheer me on.

There were two new faces in the Bruno camp: my mother Lynette and my old friend George Francis. Terry had asked George to help out. I didn't know it then, but he would be with me for the rest of my career. This was the first time my mother had seen me fight, and I knew how much she hated it. She wasn't the only one there who felt nervous.

Terry wasn't his usual cheery self. At the time, I put it down to big-night nerves. But later he told me the real reason: he didn't think I was ready. If the TV negotiations had delayed the fight, Terry wouldn't have minded too much. He wouldn't have minded, even, if they'd taken Witherspoon's title off him for failing the drugs test. It would have bought me a year for another good learning fight or two.

After I'd seen Witherspoon's flabby body at the weigh-in, I decided to go out fast. If he hadn't trained properly, and I could keep up a solid pace, he'd begin to question himself. That's what can happen during a fight. The smallest doubt becomes a big one under pressure. You can't lie to yourself. Not really. You can pretend, which is not quite the same thing. You know the truth.

Time to go to work. I said a quick prayer and we left the dressing room. The theme from *Rocky* was filling Wembley. We went through the famous tunnel, where hundreds of football teams had gone before. It took for ever to get to the ring.

For the first six rounds I've got Witherspoon where I want him. My balance is good. Everything is clicking and I can hear the crowd going crazy. I try to block out the noise – the only voices I want to listen to are in my corner – but it's impossible to ignore the cheering, not when there's so many people. My jab is finding the target and I'm doubling up behind it with a long right and a left hook. Always finish a combination with a left hook, they say. There isn't a lot coming the other way and what does get through doesn't trouble me much. I'm feeling super-confident. But I've still got an eye out for that overarm right. That's his pet finisher.

As the fight enters its second stage, though, I'm starting to tire. It can't be a stamina thing. Physically, I'm as near to perfect as I'll ever be. The problem is nerves. I'm on such a mental high, so wound up, that I'm burning up energy. I shouldn't be. I should be as loose as a goose, given how the fight has been going. But this is the night of my life. I want desperately to win it for everyone. Am I worrying too much about failing? I've got to put those thoughts out of my head and concentrate on my boxing. I'm starting to get ragged. My legs aren't taking me to the places I want to go and I'm throwing punches wildly, out of position and off balance.

It's round eight, and Witherspoon has worked his way back into the fight. That flab didn't tell the whole story. There's nothing wrong with his fitness. His corner are still going mental, but he's as cool as any dude can be. Totally professional. And smart. He senses my tiredness. He picks up the pace, putting a little more into his punches to see if I will 'go'. I'm not in trouble yet, but more of them are getting through. They're adding up. I can't get out of the way now. Terry is worried, I can tell.

'Get behind the jab again, Frank,' he says at the end of the round. 'Keep him on the end of the jab and try to stay away from that right.'

But I'm struggling. Rounds nine and ten don't go well. I'm still waiting for my second wind. It has to arrive soon, surely. Then I'll be fine. Then I'll get back into this fight and take Witherspoon out. I know I'm ahead on points but I'm not too sure what I'll be like if this goes the whole fifteen rounds. I need to knock him out.

My work's not making any impression. He keeps swaying out of range. He's stopping most of my punches, and the ones getting through aren't hurting. Why can't I find a right like the one that laid out Gerrie Coetzee? The questions are buzzing in my head. I'm filling up with self-doubt. It's draining my energy.

Then it comes back to me. At last. We're in round eleven, four from the finish line. I throw two big rights that make him blink. I've got his respect again. He moves away. He must wonder if he's taken me too lightly. I'm back in the fight. Then he counters. And how. He catches me high on the head with that chopping, overarm right. It's the punch I've been looking out for all night. But I don't see it.

My brain starts clanging. I can't focus and my gloves drop to my waist. I've stopped boxing completely. I want to hit back but I can't. I'm frozen on the spot. I'm so stunned I don't think to go down.

From somewhere, God knows where, I find some power. I fire back. But I'm so slow. I'm still out of it. I'm swinging wildly but I can't line him up for a big right. That's my only chance. He's bulldozing through my punches now. He's sizing me up for the finish. And there's nothing I can do about it. I'm drained and hurt. I can't respond. He moves inside my guard and catches me with another clubbing right. My arms slip down by my sides again. I'm a sitting duck.

There's no noise, no pain. Just a dull feeling. He's thrashing punches down on the side of my head and I'm starting to crumble. I'm sinking to the bottom rope in my own corner. Even then he doesn't stop. He's bashing me as hard as he can. I'm sagging like a rag doll. The bell goes. Terry has seen enough. He's waving the towel at the referee. He's seen enough too. That's it.

There's not a lot you can say after losing. The dressing room was like a morgue. It's not the physical pain you feel. It's the disappointment, the feeling that you've let people down.

Nobody said much. Terry gave me a hug. At least he didn't threaten to quit boxing this time.

I wasn't sure I wanted to read what the papers had to say. There would always be criticism. The fight had meant so much – to the whole country. I was their champion. But Jimmy Tibbs told reporters I had 'no natural ability'. He said I was stiff and relied too much on my jab. That was a bit harsh, seeing he'd been my trainer for six years. It was his job to coach me, wasn't it? This was our last fight together and, if that's what he thought about my boxing, maybe it was just as well.

Not everybody tore me to pieces, though. The *Sunday Times* were kind – which surprised me. They'd been on our case over 'the Cartel', especially Nick Pitt, who wrote their boxing stories. He called my loss 'a very brave failure'; I boxed 'better than we knew he could'. Along with several others Pitt reckoned my stamina and chin were suspect. I put it down to anxiety and nervousness. That's what sapped my strength and undid my concentration. I wasn't worried about my chin, though. When any heavyweight connects, believe me, it will scramble your brains.

I was more concerned about what those close to me thought than the newspaper guys. What do you say to your kids, to your partner, when you take a beating like that? What do they say to you? 'We'll get over it, Frank,' Laura said. And we would. But I still felt down. I had come through the Bonecrusher defeat OK. The stakes were much higher now though.

For ages I'd been telling Terry I wanted to test myself. I'd taken that test, and failed. Until my nerves got to me at the end, I was happy enough with my performance. But it's all about the result. And there was no getting away from it: Terrible Tim did a number on me.

Terry thought it wasn't the end of the world. The fight had come too early, and he was sure we'd get another crack at some version of the title. I was only twenty-four and the heavyweight scene was still in chaos. A week later, the fighter who would terrify the division was having his twenty-fifth contest, against Joe Frazier's son, Marvis, in Glens Falls, New York. He knocked Marvis out in thirty seconds. Within four months, Mike Tyson would be heavyweight champion of the world.

I was too down on myself. Witherspoon was better on the night, but it was just one night. Terry and Mickey told me to keep my spirits up. I'd been unlucky. After a while I started to believe them. I was still going to box – how else could I provide for the four of us? – and I was going to be world champion. I had the power.

The money helped ease the pain. I was making the big bucks that Terry and Mickey had always promised I would. Laura made sure I hung on to it. The fight put nearly $1 million in the bank. There were a fair few expenses to pay but I hadn't done badly. I was luckier than most.

Poor Tim didn't do so well. It seems incredible now, but we found out he only got $90,000 for defending his title. He chased Don King through the courts for seven years and finally got his money. But he couldn't fight for a large chunk of that time, because King held him to his contract. Tim was never 'Terrible' again.

None of that was anything to do with me. I threw the punches; the promoters and managers did the haggling. And the lawyers cleaned up. For now, it was out of my hands. My job was to put my career back together for the second time. Terry was right. This was going to be a long, tough climb to the top.

I didn't fight again for eight months. It was a relief to get away from boxing for a while – and it was great to spend some time with Laura and the kids. Nicola was four and would soon be going to school. Rachel was still a little bundle of laughs. But I couldn't totally neglect my training. When I wasn't at home I was back in the gym, working. Now that Jimmy was gone, Terry asked George to take over my training. I knew I had to do more work on my movement and my defence, but George was also going to teach me about surviving in the ring.

Terry and Mickey were out on the road, wheeling and dealing. In November, Tyson stopped Trevor Berbick in the second round to become the WBC champion. Now Iron Mike was the only show in town. He wasn't just the most intimidating heavyweight since Sonny Liston, he was born to sell tickets. Everybody made money with Mike. And I still wanted to be the best. To do that, I had to beat Tyson.

Terry and Mickey knew they could make the fight. Even though it meant another wrangle with Don King. But first I needed to prove myself all over again.

Three things pleased me about my second 'comeback': it was against a credible opponent, James 'Quick' Tillis; I won well – and Tyson was there to see it. Everyone knew that's where all this was leading. The fans at Wembley Arena were up on their feet. 'Broo-no! Broo-no!' they shouted. And the papers seemed to have forgotten about Witherspoon.

It took me just five rounds to get rid of Quick, a fighter with a good pedigree and a lot of skill. What we didn't know, before the fight, was if he still had the ambition. But I'd had his number at Grossinger's and I was confident I'd have it now. He caught me a couple of times with long rights, but I nailed him on the ropes and the fight left him. In the months since I'd lost to Witherspoon, George had made a real difference to my boxing. There'd never been a question that I could punch, but I was fighting with a bit more devil now. I was more relaxed and I had my confidence back.

I didn't feel so comfortable in my next fight. Three months later, June 1987, I was stuck in the south of France in the middle of the biggest farce of my career. Chuck Gardner was a middle-aged man – some said he might have been fifty – with some great one-liners and no boxing ability. He'd been knocked out in his previous six fights. It took me exactly one minute to do the same.

I didn't want to know about the excuses: we shouldn't have been in the same ring. I was beating up a fat comedian old enough to be my father. What good was this doing me? I was embarrassed, and disgusted. As Frank Warren said: 'Chuck Gardner? He couldn't beat my gardener.' Mike Barrett thought the fight was ludicrous. He'd just about had enough.

It didn't get much better two months later in Marbella. Reggie Gross had been fairly handy in his time. That day the big American just didn't want to know. Somehow, he lasted into the eighth before the referee called it off.

This nonsense had to stop. And it did. Sort of. I'd have one more fight before I met Tyson. My opponent had a name and a good record – he'd survived against Muhammad Ali and Joe Frazier. But the Joe Bugner I met at White Hart Lane in October 1987 was a shadow of his old self. In '83 I'd wanted this fight. Back then boxing politics had got in the way. Now Joe was a cagey 37-year-old. It seemed to me he was only there to mess me about as much as he could without getting hurt. When he slid down the ropes in the eighth, it was a relief to everyone.

It was hardly a good fight, but we both made decent money. And it let Joe grab the headlines again – which he loved. He had some kind words to say about me afterwards. 'I take my hat off to him,' he told reporters. 'He'll give Tyson plenty to think about. He certainly hit me harder than I thought he could. I think Bruno has every chance.'

But not before a long and frustrating wait.

II

Tyson

THERE'S NO GETTING AWAY FROM MIKE TYSON – INSIDE OR OUTSIDE the ring. He's been part of my life since I met him in the Catskills when I was twenty and we were a pair of young pups on the way up. He was only sixteen but he was some fighter, even then. I gave as good as I got when we sparred; I looked forward to doing it in front of a paying audience one day. Little did I know how long it would take.

After I'd beaten Joe Bugner, it all looked so easy – we were negotiating my title shot, and we were pretty confident we'd bring it to London, in front of a home crowd, the next summer. Sometimes in boxing, these deals can take ages. Besides, Mike had two fighters to get out of the way first – Tony Tubbs and Michael Spinks – and we hoped there wouldn't be an upset. But Mike's life has been one big storm – and, just as we were getting close, it blew up like Hurricane Dennis.

The story of our first contest sums up what's wrong with

boxing. If there's anyone out there who thinks it's just about two guys agreeing to fight for a title and getting in the ring, then look at how the potentially best heavyweight of all time tried to throw it all away in the space of a couple of years . . .

We agreed on terms in February 1988. I was fired up, getting ready for the biggest fight of my life. The build-up to the Witherspoon showdown had been something, but this was going to be even bigger. Forget Euro '88, forget the Seoul Olympics, this was what the country would be talking about that summer. Wembley was going to be buzzing, and this time I wasn't going to make any mistakes.

Mike didn't give a monkey's about that. Just as Terry and Mickey were getting the deal done, the guy started to go seriously off the rails. He was in deep trouble – with his managers, his wife and Don King. Not a bad trio. It was like a very bad episode of *EastEnders*.

The problems started early. It took months for the lawyers to thrash out the details. Don King was doing what he did best. He wasn't Mike's manager yet, but the two were getting closer and closer. Cus D'Amato, Mike's trainer and the man who'd been the biggest influence in his life, had died back in 1985. A couple of years later Jim Jacobs, Mike's co-manager, was struck down with leukaemia. He died in March 1988. With D'Amato and Jacobs gone, Bill Cayton, the last of the men who'd looked after Mike's career from the start, was on the way out.

As the lawyers argued, the date for our meeting was pushed back again and again. King didn't care – if the fight was in

London he wouldn't be part of the promotion. At Wembley, it belonged to Mickey and Jarvis Astaire. Don told our people that 'Bruno could be put on hold'. Mickey and Jarvis were worried: Jarvis had the stadium for 3 September, but he couldn't hold that booking for ever – Bruce Springsteen and U2 wanted that date too. As ever, nobody thought to ask me. I was simply put 'on hold'. And what could I have done anyway? Meanwhile, Mike's life was falling to pieces. He and his wife Robin were in the New York papers nearly every week. 'You're a lowlife, you're a nobody,' she told him when they went out to the theatre. She wanted him to get rid of Bill Cayton, because the manager had said bad things about her. On and on it went. But then there was hope. Mike told the press the fight was on for September, after all. Bruce and Bono would have to find another gig.

Cayton was getting fed up with King's 'trickerations'. He asked the courts to put the fight back to January so they could sort out who owned the champ. This was very bad news. We reckoned we'd sell 40,000 tickets if we had the fight outdoors in September. Any later and it might have to be moved indoors. That would mean a huge drop at the gate – and a huge drop in the purse.

And Mike had to earn some serious money. He was due $21 million from his previous contest – a quick knockout of Michael Spinks in June – but the money had been frozen because of the row between King and Cayton. It was obvious to everyone his marriage was on its last legs, and if Robin divorced him it was going to be expensive. I don't think Mike knew what was going on. Neither did we – so Jarvis flew over to try to save the Wembley show.

Things seemed to get a little clearer once Cayton and King's court case was over. Cayton remained Mike's manager of record, but really he was out, even though he'd agreed to take a big cut in his percentage. At the settlement, Tyson dissed him big time. 'He is employed by me,' he said. 'I'm not employed by him.' If I hadn't found it all so frustrating, I'd have been with Mike on this one. At least Cayton was doing his best to get Mike to London. He was offering suites at the best hotels, sixteen Concorde tickets for him and his friends, another forty on regular flights and a hell of a purse . . .

If – and it was a big if – things went ahead as planned, Mike would make $9 million. My cut, originally, was going to be $1.8 million. There was a lot of TV money involved. HBO wanted the fight in their own backyard in their own prime time, but they cut a deal: we'd be fighting in the early hours again. The BBC were paying $500,000, and that was for the right to show the fight later that day. We reckoned the gate at a sold-out Wembley would be at least £5 million. That would have made it the biggest live money event in the history of British sport. Even then, Mike wasn't impressed.

'I think I'm going to pass on the Bruno fight,' he told the papers. 'I'm going to take six or eight weeks off to relax. I don't feel like fighting right now. Please, by no means am I scared of Bruno. I just don't want to get on a plane and fly five hours, or three hours, or whatever. I want to stay in the United States.'

That really put the cat among the pigeons. If Tyson refused the contest, Mickey was going to go to the boxing authorities and ask them to strip him of his title, because I was the mandatory challenger. Then I'd fight someone else for the belt, with the winner to meet Tyson down the road. We were clutching at straws. Jarvis told the press the fight was going on in October, still outdoors. It was quite a risk.

As I went quietly up the wall in London, Mike was keeping himself busy with a little freelance work. Early – 4 a.m., the papers said – on a Tuesday in August, he got into a fight in Harlem outside a late-night clothes shop called Dapper Dan's. His opponent in the street, Mitch 'Blood' Green, had once fought him in the ring. He lost over ten rounds but put up a good show. He wanted a rematch – maybe he thought going berserk at Mike in the street was the way to get one. By all accounts, it wasn't much of a scrap. But Mike broke his hand on the other guy's head.

Now it looked like October was off the menu too. I couldn't believe it. I was in and out of training like a yo-yo. Amazingly, Tyson was back in the gym a couple of weeks later. Maybe we were going to fight in London after all. Not quite. He crashed his car into a tree at his Catskills training camp and was unconscious for about twenty minutes. He wasn't badly hurt, but the doctors said he couldn't train for a month. That really put the kibosh on October.

Jarvis told reporters the fight was still on – you could prob-ably have heard the laughter in the Catskills – and that we'd hold Tyson to his contract. Now it was going indoors at Wembley on 16 December.

While Mike was in hospital, a New York newspaper came out with a sensational story. They claimed that before the crash he'd phoned his wife to tell her he was going to kill himself – after killing her. It was all nonsense. But there were obviously problems between them. It turns out she had been trying to get him to see a psychiatrist. How familiar that would sound to me – and Mike – ten years later.

It got worse for Tyson. He and Robin were due to go to Moscow – Robin was an actress, and they were shooting a couple of episodes of her sitcom in Russia. Mike lost it before they got on the plane. And he didn't stay long either. He got homesick after a week, and left. I think the fact that Robin's mother turned up didn't help. Trapped in a lousy Moscow hotel with the mother-in-law was probably not Mike's idea of a holiday.

Tyson was getting wilder by the day, screaming at everyone who came near him. If we ever did get to fight I had no idea what sort of man I would be facing. When he and Robin gave a TV interview together, he said he'd been hyperactive all his life but he wasn't 'a psychopath or a maniac'. I knew a little about him and I reckon he was right. We both suffered from an excess of energy. And, in different ways, both of us cracked.

Then Robin put the boot in. She told the interviewer that life with Mike was a nightmare. He was scary and often lost his temper. And, she said, he was a 'manic depressive'. I don't know how Mike stood for it, to be honest. He obviously still loved Robin. Maybe he didn't understand what she was saying. Normally he's very sharp, but he just sat there while his wife made a total fool of him in front of millions of people.

His wife and mother-in-law, his old manager, his new manager – they were fighting over him like a piece of meat. Is it any wonder he was behaving strangely? He finally went to a psychiatrist, who said he wasn't a manic depressive. I imagine Mike didn't know who to believe. Years later, a psychiatric team would claim he had 'chronic depression'. That's not the same as my bipolar disorder, and in fact the doctors said he wasn't mentally ill at all, but he was still very troubled. He was on a mood stabiliser called Zoloft for years.

Robin filed for divorce in October and I thought, well, that's that; Mike's going to be tied up in court for ages. But Mickey had some half-decent news, for once. Tyson was back in training. I didn't get my hopes up. Apparently he was still about seventeen stone. Normally, he weighed in at about fifteen and a half stone before a fight. I'd believe I was fighting Mike Tyson the night I looked across the ring and saw him in the other corner. Same as always.

I was right. Tyson hurt his hand again – sparring this time – and December was off. It was back to New York for Jarvis and Mickey. I told them to make it clear to Tyson's people I wanted the fight in London. I wanted to win the world title in front of my own fans, in my own city. So they flew me out to tell the American papers just that in person. I did, but I can't imagine it made any difference to Tyson. He was making me angrier by the day. I was so wound up I started to lose my temper, which I rarely do. I thought he was disrespecting the title. And he was disrespecting me.

The last straw was when Mike announced he was signing with Don King. We had yet another new date – 14 January – but I reckoned now there was no chance at all of Tyson coming to London. Don didn't have a piece of the fight – but he would if we fought in Las Vegas. They'd put me on hold right enough. I thought I'd been stupid promising to sign with two managers when I started my boxing career; at least

I had the excuse that I was eighteen. Tyson was even more naive than I'd been. King called him 'my partner'. Right.

By my count, the fight had been postponed five times. I felt like I was going to be in training for the rest of my life. Then we had the news we'd been waiting so long for. The fight was on. For definite. And it was only a year after we'd signed the original contracts. But Mike and I were just about the only part of the deal that had stayed the same. Don King would be in on the promotion, and we'd be meeting 8,000 miles from Wembley: at the Las Vegas Hilton on 25 February 1989.

Mike's life may have been a bigger disaster than *The Towering Inferno*, but none of his shenanigans helped me. I hadn't had a fight since October 1987. I wanted to give myself every chance of winning the world title and the stop-start training just mucked me about. Getting the timing right is one of the secrets of success in boxing, especially at the highest level. It's a very hard thing to do when your fight's called off every other day.

'This is not right,' George Francis kept telling me. 'You've probably peaked five times. Your weight's all over the place – fifteen and a half to sixteen and a half stone. We've got to start again and make sure we get everything spot on. No room for error, Frank.'

George was a master at getting me ready. It was all about trust. He was the sort of guy who would just shake hands on a deal. He didn't want to sign anything. And you could count on George not to go running off to the papers.

'Frank,' he used to say, 'never trust people who want to be

your friend when you're winning. When you're on top, you're everybody's mate. But they only want to get close because of the title, the money, the fame. They couldn't care less about the real Frank Bruno.' It was sound advice. George, like myself, was a bit of a loner. He wasn't distant or rude. He just didn't want to be sucked in by strangers. I couldn't have asked for a better trainer – or a better friend.

I was loyal to George because he was a good man. Money wasn't the be-all and end-all of things for him. I tried to look after him, financially. I hope I did. Once he got to like you, you couldn't help but like him. We enjoyed each other's company and that's not always the case in boxing. But he would have made a fierce enemy. He was as hard as nails, a no-nonsense sort of bloke.

You had to be tough where George grew up, in Camden Town in north London. He went out to work when he was eleven, because his father had died. He became a porter at Covent Garden market, the old one, and I understand he was a decent amateur boxer. But training was what he was really good at because he had a generous spirit. He wanted to pass on knowledge. Look at the champions he had: John Conteh, John Mugabe, Cornelius Boza-Edwards. Not to mention a whole load of other black fighters nobody wanted at the time. As everyone in the game knows, George did a lot to break down prejudice in boxing. There was a time in Britain when you had to be white and born here to fight for a British title. George hated all that. His hero was another fighter against racism, Paul Robeson, the singer and actor.

If it wasn't for George, fighters like Lenny Gibbs and Bunny

Sterling, two of his favourites, might never have made a living in the game. George told me how in his early days promoters wouldn't put them on their shows. 'Black fighters didn't sell then, Frank,' he'd say. It was one of the reasons I didn't like the comments about me playing the white man's game with Terry and Mickey. Terry had plenty of black fighters. I don't think those guys saw colour – except the colour of money. When it turned out that I could pack out Wembley or the Royal Albert Hall, Mickey was more than happy to push my career. And I did what I was asked to do to sell tickets. Because I remembered what George had told me, that once nobody would look twice at a black fighter in this country. If I helped open up the market, well and good. And, of course, I was in it for the money too.

George believed in me. Not everyone did. Throughout my career, boxing writers and even some of my fans were torn between supporting me and fearing I was going to get killed. All year the headlines made grim reading. I could understand it. People forget how awesome Tyson was back then. He was twenty-three and had been tearing through the heavyweight division for a little over four years. Only four of his thirty-five victims had made it to the final bell. He'd knocked out all the others – sixteen of them in the first round. By far the most stunning win of his career was in his fight against Michael Spinks, eight months before we met. If you saw that fight, you won't need reminding of the image of a petrified Spinks being blown away in ninety-one seconds. I certainly remembered it. But, as I got ready for Tyson, I had to put all that out of my head.

Of course, I felt nervous. Every boxer does before a big

fight. But this was my job. I'd learnt to control fear. I used it to make me train harder, to give myself the best chance against the best heavyweight we'd seen since Muhammad Ali. There were people saying then that Tyson might become the best of all time. And I was going to share a ring with him. If I wasn't nervous, I wasn't alive. But I'm sure Mike was nervous too. He knew all about my power. He'd felt a little bit of it when we sparred back in '82 and I hoped to remind him how hard I could hit in a proper fight.

All I heard from the experts was that I lacked a 'killer instinct'. George set about changing that. He wasn't just a terrific trainer, he knew how to work on your mind. 'Frank,' he said, 'there's going to be no more Mr Nice Guy. You know, I know, and the whole world knows that Tyson will use every trick in the book to win. If he can get away with it – even if he can't – he'll use his elbows, his head, he'll push and shove you like it's a street fight. That's what this is going to be, Frank, and you've got to be ready for it.'

George taught me a few tricks of his own. He showed me how to put an opponent off balance at the right moment with a little shove and then climb into him legally; he made me bear down on the necks of my sparring partners to tire them out. And he told me something else about what to do in the heat of battle.

'If you're hurt, go down. Take a knee, clear your head and, when you get up, hang on to him for dear life.'

It was good advice. I should have listened more closely, but it went against my instincts. I'm not Mr Goody-Two-Shoes in the ring. Far from it – as the world would see when I got in the ring with Mike. But I like to think a fight is decided between two boxers giving everything they've got. I looked on taking a count as not right. The same with hanging on when you're trying to clear your head. I wanted to stand and trade. It was my way. I wanted to knock them out and go home.

'It's not giving up, Frank,' George would say. 'It's clever. All the great boxers have done it. Muhammad Ali was a master at messing his opponents about. Rocky Marciano was one of the dirtiest fighters in the business. And he never lost.'

When we finally got the date, George and I headed off to Fountain Hills, near Phoenix, Arizona. Mike was training at Johnny Tocco's gym in Las Vegas, where the champions worked out. He was even staying in Don King's house. You could tell who was the favoured fighter in this deal. I wasn't bothered. I was here to work. I had six weeks to turn every problem to my use. I didn't need extra motivation, but I had plenty. I was very wound up about Tyson. It was up to me to make the best use of that anger.

George put together the toughest training programme of my career. It was hell. But that's what I loved, pushing myself to the limit. It made me strong. I felt I could knock down a house. For all his faults, Tyson was a pretty fierce trainer too. But he'd let himself go completely between fights and then work extra hard to get back into shape. He was just about small enough to get away with such dodgy training.

I wanted every edge I could get. I even hired a hypnotist, a guy from Las Vegas called David Silverman. I know it sounds a bit odd, but you take whatever you can if you think it'll help you win. I reckoned I was ahead of my time on this one – then I found out Mike had his own man, John Halpin. It was one all in mind games, then.

I'd looked deep into Dr Silverman's eyes, done more miles than Seb Coe and I was belting the granny out of my sparring partners. I knew I'd be in the greatest shape of my life on fight night. As long as I could dodge one particular admirer . . .

I was relaxing in the hotel lobby in Fountain Hills when this loud, redneck woman came over. She sat down and put her legs across mine. Funny way to say hello, I thought. She was probably in her late twenties and she was a big, big woman. Not fat. Solid. She looked like she'd give you a proper argument. And I didn't think she wanted to talk about the fight.

'I want your babies,' she said. I didn't know how to take it. At first I thought she was joking, or maybe she was having a go at me. But when she started chasing me round the hotel, turning up at all hours, I worked out she was serious. It sounds like a laugh, but I was there to work. I had a meeting with the toughest man on the planet in a matter of weeks.

Something had to be done. If I talked to her it would make things worse. So George had to have a word.

'Can't carry on like this, George. She's putting me off my training.'

'OK. I'll handle it.'

He laid it on the line. Either she left me alone or he'd tell her guv'nor. That seemed to do it. George was a streetwise guy, and he could spot someone on the make a mile away.

Boxers do attract women. Look at Tyson. But you've got to

be on your guard because, usually, they want one of two things: sex or money. Sometimes both, if they can sell their story to the papers. If you're a faithful sort of guy, you're not interested on either count.

I was old-fashioned in my preparation, and I stayed away from the bedroom for at least a month before a big fight. I know some people say it's nonsense to think that sex can drain you. Maybe it is. But it's a psychological thing, not physical. It's about keeping your mind on the fight. You wake up in the morning – you're thinking about the fight. Before you go to sleep – you're thinking about the fight. For a couple of months of your life, nothing else matters. That's why I could have done without all this fuss.

Then again, if I'd had no sex at all getting ready for this particular fight, I'd have been crawling up the wall. It was postponed so many times I was in training for the best part of a year.

In 1989, Mike still had the fire in him. And so did I. George had given me every chance: I was at my physical peak and I was ready to tear the ring posts down to get at Tyson. In my mind, the title was there for the taking. It would be a huge job. I'd been out of the ring for sixteen months – eight months longer than Tyson. Normally, a fighter would be worried about being rusty after such a long break. But I wasn't, oddly enough. I had so much energy, I desperately needed an outlet. Knocking Mike Tyson out to win the world title was the perfect way to get rid of my frustrations. I was like a volcano.

Thanks to all Mike's troubles, we'd ended up with a smaller

pot. He was only going to get $3 million, a third of what Bill Cayton had originally promised him for a trip to London. My cut was about a third of that. But I'd put all that out of my mind. I wanted that title more than breathing. There'd be some verbals before we got in the ring, though.

The trash talk before the fight was the worst I'd ever come across. And the eyeballing at the weigh-in was pretty special too. Sometimes I got sick of this side of our business. Ninety-nine per cent of it was garbage, but that never stopped the papers printing every word of it. It puts bums on seats, it does the job – but, as far as I was concerned, it just used up valuable time. I never spoke badly about my opponents, and I couldn't understand how they could have a go at me. You usually didn't know the guy you were fighting from Adam, anyway, let alone hate him. And nine times out of ten, you could be sure it was the promoter or someone else egging him on. What you had to do, though, was put the other guy at the front of your mind. For the weeks leading up to a fight – especially this one – my opponent was on my mind nearly every waking hour.

I'd always had a good personal relationship with Mike. He'd rant and rave at everyone else but, with me, he was different. And I think that made him feel vulnerable. He never liked to be too close to anyone for too long, let alone the man who was trying to take his title off him.

He's a very deep character, Mike. He grew up in one of the worst ghettos in America, Brownsville. He hung out with the Jolly Stompers, a charming collection of young muggers who went after anyone who was weak. That's where he learnt to be a bully. That's where he learnt all his tricks.

Mike knows how to manipulate people, how to draw them in, to make them feel sorry for him, to make them ready for the kill. He wants to be your friend before he mugs you. It makes his job easier. It's a street thing. He's a very, very clever guy. So when the trash talk stopped and Mike started sounding like he was my brother, I knew it was for a reason. 'I think Frank is a really nice guy,' he said. 'He is so well mannered and so respectful. Whenever we've met, I've never heard him bad-mouth anyone . . . There is no way I would want to hurt him or bust him up.'

You could see the left hook coming off the jab. 'That's why, for the sake of his family as well as himself, I will take him out in the opening round. He knows I always try to get a fight over as quickly as possible. Just as he does. It's the nature of our business. But I have a special reason for getting it over quickly where he is concerned: he's such a sweet man.'

Look closely at those words, and you'll understand a lot about Mike Tyson. There's the man who cares. It's not just an act. Then there's the total professional, who knows he has to get a job done and wants to get out of the place as soon as he can. That's also genuine. (Most fighters, especially heavy-weights, hate hanging about – every new round is a new danger.) And then there's Tyson the master of mind games.

Once, there was nobody better in boxing than Mike at breaking an opponent down mentally. As good as Ali, except not so funny. He wants you to crap yourself. It's what Cus D'Amato told him years earlier in the Catskills: use fear, don't let fear use you. When Mike talked in that quiet, high-pitched lisp, you had to listen closely to what he was saying.

Mike also went to work on his own mind. He'd go easy

on his training at the start, scaring himself into thinking the other guy was in better shape. It was how he motivated himself. He knew, too, that people didn't like him – that they hated him, even – and he drew on that as well. 'I've been by myself all my life,' he would say. 'I've been abused. I've been dehumanised. I've been humiliated. I've been betrayed.'

All of that was true. And Mike pointed to it over and over again to make people feel sorry for him. Then he'd tell the do-gooders that real men don't have pity. Real men are too hard for that. Except he knew, deep down, it wasn't true. It was his front. His act. And, for most of his crazy career, he pulled it off brilliantly. Nobody knew what to make of Mike. Least of all Mike.

At his best, he was some fighter, and, despite all his problems, he was still near his best in 1989. Bookmakers were even making him odds on to break Rocky Marciano's unbeaten run of 49–0. Mike was the biggest name in sport. Anywhere. Once his weaknesses had been exposed, though, he slowly fell apart. He had nobody. Cus D'Amato and Jim Jacobs were dead. Bill Cayton was virtually out. His wife had left him. All he had was a bunch of 'new friends'. Mike always said it would be like that. He was a smart man . . . and very, very sad. As he used to say, 'Old too soon, smart too late.'

I like Mike. I haven't spoken to him in a long time, but there is a bond there, like there is between all fighters. I wouldn't say we were bosom buddies, but I have no hard feelings towards Mike and I hope he feels the same way. When he fought Lou Savarese in Glasgow a few years ago, I tried to get to see him – but there were too many minders in the way. That's the sort of life he has, surrounded by his 'new friends'.

But in February of 1989, I had to make him my enemy for a night. No matter what we felt about each other, our job was fighting. And fights don't get bigger than the world heavyweight title. If I ever wondered why I was in this business, it was nights like this that reminded me.

I2

Leaving Las Vegas

THE FIGHT WAS SHORT – FIVE ROUNDS – AND BRUTAL.

I'd been waiting sixteen months for this moment. As I walked to the ring, I knew I'd have to fight better than I'd ever done before. I'd never been so up for anything. The atmosphere was incredible. There were thousands of Brits in the crowd – but a lot of the American fans were behind me too. They'd turned on Tyson – just like they turned on his hero, Sonny Liston, years before. He was one bad dude. But, as with Sonny, the fans couldn't look away. Mike was pure violence.

Terry walked just behind me as we pushed through the throng. There was tension between us, but we'd have to forget about that for now. I was feeding off the energy of the crowd. It seemed to leave them and enter me. It was running through my veins. I was sweated up, but I wasn't going to rush in like a four-round novice – not against the man who had two of the quickest fists in heavyweight history. I stepped through the ropes. At last. Back where I felt at home.

We look across at each other, giving nothing away. I've been through this moment already – under hypnosis. I see it in slow motion: Tyson comes at me like a lion, I steady him with a jab. I hold him off, wear him down . . . and knock him out.

Maybe Tyson has the better hypnotist: after eleven seconds he lands a bomb on my temple. My legs give way and I go down. I'm more stunned than badly hurt. I look over to George. He's mouthing something. Can't hear him. But I know what he's saying. Take the eight count, Frank. This is when Tyson's at his most dangerous, when he smells blood. I try to clear my head – and I get up straight away. I could have stayed down a little longer, maybe, like George told me to. I'm back on my feet, I grab on to him for dear life. At least I've remembered to tie him up.

'Watch the rabbit punching, Bruno,' Richard Steele says. He's one of the best referees in the world. I don't listen. I'll do anything to avoid being blown away. George has done his job well – I'm surviving. I put in two more blows to Tyson's neck. The referee deducts a point. It doesn't matter. The winner of this one is going to have an early night, whichever way it goes.

Within seconds, I give Mike the shock of his career. Nobody has really rocked him before. He still has the aura. They say you can't hurt him, that he's superhuman. Nonsense. Anyone'll go if he's hit right. I stand my ground, look for an opening. My jab's working and Tyson backs off. This is my moment. I get inside and let loose a short right. It opens him up for one of the best left hooks I've ever thrown. I can feel the shockwaves up my arms and down to my boots. In the middle of this, I hear a familiar voice. 'Get stuck in, Frank.' It's Harry Carpenter.

I've got him! He sways like a drunk. He's hanging over my shoulders like he wants me to put him in a cab back to Brownsville. But I can't get my arms free. Steele steps in, separates us and the chance is gone. Tyson has recovered. He's in some shape. There's nothing wrong with his chin, that's for sure.

In the second, I catch him with another left hook. I want to line him up for a big right but I can't get set. He's slipping my jab and I'm not fast enough to get out of the way of his counters. He's so quick. He's throwing combinations a featherweight would be proud of. He hurts me with a right. I hold on. He's taken away my boxing; we're six minutes into the fight and I'm just surviving.

I put a decent jab on him at the start of the third. But he's all over me again. Steele yells at me to stop holding. Tyson lands a short right as we break. Steele lets it pass.

Round four is worse. A long, sweeping right has my brain spinning. Again I hold. I try to get my jab going but Mike butts me. This time, Steele cautions him. I can't keep him off. He's flying. He's on top. Totally. I've got to find something. Fast.

My corner's looking worried. Terry says, 'Keep jabbing, Frank. When Tyson comes in hooking, catch him with an uppercut.' It's not that easy. If anything, Mike's getting stronger. The punches are coming from everywhere. I want to get into the fight – but Tyson's all over me. I hang on. Steele gives me my last warning. One more and I'm out of the fight. It's a terrible way to lose a world title fight: disqualified. I want to go down fighting. I'm giving it all I have – but it's not enough.

He backs me up with head shots that rattle my brain. I'm on the ropes, gloves up. I can hardly breathe. The bombs keep coming. My legs are starting to go. Out of the corner of my eye I see Terry waving a white towel. I don't want this. I really don't want this. I want to go down fighting. Then Steele steps in. He looks in my eyes, waves his hands and turns towards Tyson. It's over.

'Great fight, Frank,' Mike says.

'Thanks. A lot.'

There's nothing to say. The adrenalin's still pumping, but I'm empty. All that work – a year and a half – for this. I thought I had a good chance of beating the odds. Nobody else did. Then, after the TV interviews, as Tyson leaves the ring with his belt, his million hangers-on, and Don King, I'm there. Just me, Terry and George. I hear the fans still singing my name – 'Broo-no! Broo-no!' I've let them down. Again.

Two hours later, in the hotel room, I was as down as I'd ever been. Laura and I just sat there, talking about the future. I'd fought as well as I could but Tyson still had plenty in the tank. More than enough. I'd lost to Bonecrusher, I'd lost to Tim Witherspoon. Both times I'd been leading, and I'd put those defeats down to inexperience. I was only twenty-four when Witherspoon beat me. In 1989, I was more seasoned and had one of the finest trainers in the business in my corner. But George couldn't throw the punches for me, and I couldn't get out of the way of Tyson's. I was devastated.

In any fight, there's going to be a loser. And it's never easy to accept it – to admit the other guy's a better man. It's when all the kidding stops. I thought my big right hand might win me the title, but Tyson was a buzz saw and he cut me to pieces. He was the better man.

When you lose, you're suddenly all alone. People around you say the right things, but they can't know how bad you feel unless they've been through it themselves. There's nothing like it. You can't share your humiliation with anyone. It was all down to you, and you weren't good enough. It's not disgrace – especially if you've given as good as you've got – it's more disappointment, and it won't go away. It's as if it was all for nothing. There are no second places in boxing, no silver medals. I never thought of myself as a loser – but I'd lost three times now. I had to stop and think very carefully about where I went from here.

'That might be it for a while, Laura,' I said. 'I think I need a rest from this business. Maybe for good.' From memory, she wasn't too unhappy. But I knew she'd leave the decision to me.

George knocked, and came in. I wondered if he'd try to talk me out of quitting. Typically, he didn't interfere. He always wanted what was best for me. 'It's up to you, Frank,' he said. George didn't waste time on words. He looked at my swollen face and smiled. 'You know something, Frank?' he said as he turned to leave. 'You fought a hell of a fight tonight. A hell of a fight.'

That cheered me up no end. George wasn't the sort of person to just say that. If George Francis said I fought a hell of a fight, I fought a hell of a fight.

But right now, I didn't want to think about the fight. I just wanted to get out of Vegas. There's nowhere worse than the scene of the crime after you've lost. And what would everyone be saying back home?

I couldn't believe the reception when we got to London. We walked through arrivals at Heathrow airport and there were thousands of people waiting. All of them cheering their heads off. Nobody seemed to mind that I'd lost. It was a strange feeling. I felt guilty for enjoying it because I'm a professional sportsman. I didn't think I deserved it. But I was really moved by their support.

Five months later, Tyson blew away Carl 'The Truth' Williams in the first round. Williams was a good boxer but he obviously wasn't up for the fight. It was probably the last time we saw a totally awesome Tyson in the ring. Soon after, he was picked up for brawling and speeding. He was drinking heavily, partying until all hours. And, since the break-up of his marriage, there was nobody there to stop him. A year after we fought, Buster Douglas knocked him out in Tokyo. It was one of boxing's greatest upsets. I wasn't as surprised as most people.

I had problems of my own – not quite as bad as Mike's, but bad enough. Things hadn't been going so well between Terry and me for a while. It was mainly to do with the Tyson fight, all the delays, all the mucking about. I was bound to blow my top every now and again. But there was something else, something that went much deeper.

Terry and I had been together for ten years. We'd been like father and son once. I remembered the early days, the meals his wife Sylvia would cook for me up at their place in Essex. I'd been friends with his son Stephen and his daughter Lorraine. I even listened to Terry's Pavarotti collection – although I stopped short of reading his books on Zen.

I know Terry cared. He was in tears after I lost to Bonecrusher. But there are all sorts of pressures in professional boxing. And they usually have to do with control. Terry and Mickey made it clear at the start of my career that they were in charge. I accepted that. If I asked about contracts or that side of it, I'd be told to leave it to them. They were investing in me, they said. And they knew best.

But I'd grown up. I'd matured. I wanted to be in control of my life. I wasn't the raw kid from Wandsworth any more. I'd seen quite a bit in ten years. I'd learnt a little about the game. So, we argued. Things had changed. Terry didn't sub me any more. My fights made millions of pounds. And I was the one in the ring. Not Terry. Not Mickey. Not Jarvis – or anyone else. I wasn't an employee any more.

Laura had got more involved in the business side of it, which suited me. It got a bit personal and there was a lot of tension. Terry and I had had so many good nights. It was better to split now before it got too ugly.

I had to give Terry credit for what he'd done. I was grateful to him. I still am – I couldn't have done it without him –

though I don't know how much he believed that when things got bad. He was totally honest – unlike some in the fight game. Now, though, we'd reached the end of the road.

Boxing is full of arguing. If it wasn't me and Terry, it was Terry and Frank Warren, or Mickey and Frank Warren, or Frank and someone else. Or Barry Hearn and Mickey. Or Barry and Frank. Mad. It's just the way it is. Yet I had good times with nearly all of them. They lived a different life to me. They seemed to thrive on aggravation. I walked away from it. Some fighters can't handle the pressure outside the ring, all the wrangling. My way was to keep a sense of humour about the whole crazy business.

But we're both adults, Terry and me. He's a pretty resilient character. Also, we'd made a lot of corn. And we'd had a lot of laughs. Not many laughs that last night together, though. Terry was gutted. So was I. But there were more important things in life than boxing.

It was good to get back to Hornchurch and just be a family again for a while. My career had hit a low point and it was time to rebuild. Laura and I were now in business together; Nicola and Rachel were turning into lovely kids. I felt better about life. It was time to make another big decision. Laura and I were getting married.

'Nice to hear it, Franklin,' Mum said. I knew it would please her.

The wedding was wonderful, a day to remember. Father Tony McSweeney, the local priest, took the service. My brother Michael was best man and the band played 'Tell Laura I Love Her'. There were hundreds of guests and we couldn't move for wedding presents. There was even a set of silver napkin rings from Prince Charles and Princess Diana. Outside the church, thousands of people turned up to wish us well. We were as happy as any two people have a right to be. And we never imagined it wouldn't last.

13

Lennox and Me

IT'S NO SECRET THAT I HAVEN'T ALWAYS GOT ON WITH LENNOX LEWIS. It's about self-respect. It's about identity and pride. It's about my place as a black Briton, a representative of my community. And it's about how he disrespected me.

When Lennox arrived from Canada, he seemed like a nice enough guy. He was laid-back, well-mannered. He didn't make loud noises about conquering the world. He said he was happy to be back in the town he called home.

Lennox had won the superheavyweight title at the 1988 Olympics for Canada and, understandably, he was hot property. There were several people who wanted to sign him, here and in America. Even Mickey Duff showed an interest. Lennox was no fool. He knew Britain was desperate for a world heavyweight champion. (He obviously hadn't taken much notice of my career.) If he fought in Canada, where he'd lived since the age of eleven, or in the States, he wouldn't have the same selling power; big heavyweights were a dime a dozen over there – although, to be fair to Lennox, not many were as good as he was.

Lennox was born in the heart of London's East End and sold himself as a cockney. He said he'd climbed over the turnstiles at Upton Park as a young boy to watch his beloved Hammers. I'm not saying he didn't. It just didn't sound that convincing in a Canadian accent.

Four months after I got back from Las Vegas, Lennox made his professional debut – at the Albert Hall. His two-round victim was Al Malcolm – followed by five more fights just as easy that year. So, in the time-honoured tradition, he was being built up as a contender – just as I had been. After the setback against Tyson, I had to start again – and I knew that one day I'd end up in the ring with Lewis. What I didn't know then was I'd have to wait four years and go through more hell to get to him . . .

All my career, I'd been lucky with injuries. I'd never been badly cut, never pulled out of a fight, never had trouble with my hands. But there wasn't much I could do about the weakness in my right eye. It had almost cost me my livelihood before I'd even started. Now I discovered I might have to quit when I should be reaching my peak. Mike Tyson had given me my third defeat – and something I hadn't bargained for: when I got home and went for my routine medical, I was gutted to find out I had a tear on my right eye.

Laura and my mother weren't so upset. I think they wanted me to retire anyway. I discussed it for ages with Laura. Since the split with Terry, I'd taken control of my life. But it wasn't just me. Laura and I were partners. Still, it was hard to accept that the decision might be taken out of our hands. If I had a dodgy eye, the board wouldn't give me a licence. Simple as that.

I had to get on with life, though. So I decided I'd have another go at acting. Well, that's what I like to call it. Four years earlier, I'd had a little stint with Lenny Henry. My comeback performance that Christmas was *Aladdin* with Michael Barrymore at the Dominion in Tottenham Court Road. It was my great honour to deliver the immortal lines: 'Here I am firm as a rock, I'm Sweenie the genie, What's up, doc?' It wasn't exactly Shakespeare.

I got to work with loads of good people in those days: Les Dawson, Freddie Starr, Frank Carson, Norman Wisdom, Cannon and Ball, Geoffrey Durham – Victoria Wood's husband at the time – Little and Large, Anne Nolan of the Nolan Sisters. In 1990 I was even offered a part in *Rocky V*. That didn't work out, but I had plenty on my plate anyway.

The main man was Harry. Since we'd hooked up at the Jumbo Cummings fight, we'd earned a fair bit of corn together on the after-dinner circuit. He was a total professional. I appeared on his *This Is Your Life* in 1991. He did the same for me two years later.

I'd gone into boxing looking to make some decent money and to be a world champion. By 1989, I'd lost three times but I couldn't walk down the street without someone calling out my name. It's a funny thing, celebrity. It seemed I was more popular than ever. Maybe people felt sorry for me. They had no reason to. I was happy enough.

After a while, people knew me for dressing up in panto

and doing ads for HP Sauce, not my boxing. My life had changed completely – the black kid from south London had even been to Buckingham Palace to pick up an MBE. But I didn't go looking for fame – I'd rather have a quiet night at home than be out on the town. I do like mixing with people, but there's only so much of yourself you can give.

Some people thought I'd given boxing up for good. They'd see me onstage playing the clown, and have a go at me in the papers. They said I was demeaning myself. I didn't think much of their opinions. This was my life and I would lead it the way I wanted to.

But what I really wanted to do was box. In 1991 I went back to David McLeod, the specialist who sorted me out when I was eighteen. David was a professor now – I wasn't the only one who'd moved on since 1980 – but, good as it was to see him again, this was no social visit. I wanted to know if I had any chance of fighting again. He said he'd do what he could. He confirmed I had a tear on my retina and I'd need surgery.

Two months after the diagnosis, I had an operation in Manchester. It was over in an hour and, thankfully, it was successful. The papers were still on my case, though – they were making all sorts of gloomy predictions. Nobody wanted me to risk going blind. As usual, nobody had a clue what they were talking about. A month later David said I was fit to box. The board agreed. I was back in the boxing business.

We moved into a new house in Stondon Massey. It seemed everything was changing. I decided I needed a high-profile promoter. I'd split with Terry but there was only so much we could do ourselves. Barry Hearn was a good, flashy frontman, the sort of ticket seller we were looking for. Barry had made his name in snooker, and pretty much ran the sport. Now he was keen to get into boxing. I was impressed.

Then Mickey Duff got in touch and my world was turned upside down again. I was never really close to Mickey but I always respected him. He had the connections, and more experience in the business than Barry. Whatever had happened between me and Terry, it didn't take Mickey long to convince me to stay with him as my promoter.

It didn't take much longer to decide on my first opponent – a Dutchman called John Emmen. On 20 November 1991 I was back in the Albert Hall, where it had all started. I'd been out for thirty-three months. Emmen, unfortunately, wasn't much of a test. He was a fitness instructor by trade and not that big. He went over in a round and the papers were on my back again. It was like the old days. I felt justified in easing myself back into the game with a short night's work – but I knew my next opponent had to be better.

The following April, I fought the Cuban Jose Ribalta at Wembley Arena. Ribalta had a good pedigree – he'd lost narrowly to a couple of old opponents of mine, Tim Witherspoon and Bonecrusher Smith. And he'd taken Tyson to ten hard rounds.

The trash talking before the fight was terrible. Ribalta sank as low as you can get. He was going to blind me, he said. It wasn't a clever wind-up. I belted the living daylights out of him for two rounds.

The fight told me I still had the hunger and I still had the punch. Now I needed the opponent. The man I wanted was Lennox Lewis. While I'd been out he'd racked up nineteen wins. The week after I beat Ribalta, Lewis won the Commonwealth title when he stopped Derek Williams. The previous year, Lewis had finished the career of my old friend and sparring partner, Gary Mason. I was there that night and it was a sad occasion. Gary had to retire from boxing with a detached retina.

It's a very common injury in boxing. It was one of the reasons Professor McLeod didn't like boxing. Every time you take a punch in that part of your head, you risk all sorts of damage – to your eyes, your brain. But we know that when we start out. If boxing went underground, David and his colleagues would be very busy men indeed. With the right controls and checks, sanctioned professional boxing is as safe as it can be. In fact, we have so many check-ups we know much more about our bodies than most people.

Obviously Lewis and I wouldn't meet before one of us had a world title. That would be dumb business. First, I'd have to get back into the top ten and, to do that, I'd have to beat fighters rated above me. First up was Pierre Coetzer, a tall South African with a great chin. We met at Wembley in October 1992 and it took me eight grinding rounds to get rid of him. I had never weighed as much – 17st 6lb – and I was sluggish. It took me four rounds just to warm up. I kept swinging – and missing. I knew it was one of my poorer performances. I caught up with him eventually and put him away with an uppercut and a pair of rights. It was a relief when his corner threw in the towel.

Two weeks later, Lewis beat Razor Ruddock in a WBC eliminator. But when Riddick Bowe refused to defend the title against Lewis, they stripped him and gave the belt to Lennox.

That March, while Lewis was getting ready to fight Tony Tucker in his first defence, I was lined up with Carl Williams. Williams was much tougher than Coetzer. He had class, and a good record. He may not have been able to live with Mike Tyson – he was blown away in a round – but back in 1989, who could? I knew yet again that everything was on the line. I was thirty-one now. If I made a mess of things, that would be it for me. No Lewis, no career, back to panto.

I was a stone and a half lighter than I had been against Coetzer and I'd worked much harder on my conditioning. I was sharper but still not back to my best. I got cut above the eye in the third and it interfered with my boxing. A tame affair finally came to the end in the tenth when I caught Williams with a right to the side of the head and he keeled over.

Two months later Lewis beat Tucker. Everything was falling into place.

If I thought Lewis was going to be the perfect gentleman in the run-up to our fight, I couldn't have been more wrong. He didn't sound like the mild-mannered guy who'd arrived in London four years earlier. He was trash-talking like all the others.

There was a lot of hype. To be fair, I played my part. It was all about our roots. He went on about being a Londoner, which I found hard to take. I was born and bred here after all. But when the papers said he'd called me an Uncle Tom

I blew my top. He denied it but I got my lawyer, Henri Brandman, to issue him with a writ for libel. Things calmed down later, and we withdrew it; but I had to let him know he couldn't take liberties. The papers thought it was a stunt – but I was deadly serious. To be accused of sucking up to the white man – I can't tell you what an insult that is. It goes to the heart of who I am.

Who was Lennox to come into my town and talk like that about me? As far as I was concerned, he didn't know a thing about my background, about the people I hung out with, about my lifestyle. If he was interested, he could have asked a couple of what he might consider 'hard-core' guys, good friends of mine like Lloyd 'Ragamuffin Man' Honeyghan and Nigel Benn.

I'd heard some of this crap before – when I took up with Laura, when I was starting out with Terry and Mickey. People said – but never to my face – that I had sold out to a group of white guys, that I was lording it up in a big mansion in Essex with my white wife. They said I wasn't 'street' enough. Ask anyone I grew up with. I was very connected to my roots. I know my culture. And I've never forgotten where I come from.

What made it twice as bitter for me was I'd never thought of Lennox as British. He may have come back now and again but he grew up in Canada. He sounds like a Canadian. To me, he *is* a Canadian. He won an Olympic gold medal, and good luck to him. The Olympics are about doing it for your country – and millions of Canadians must have been very proud of him.

This is not being stupid about it. It's a serious point. I was

(*bove*) Photographer
m Jenkins captures me
a quiet moment in the
m; and (*right*) on the
ad with George Francis.

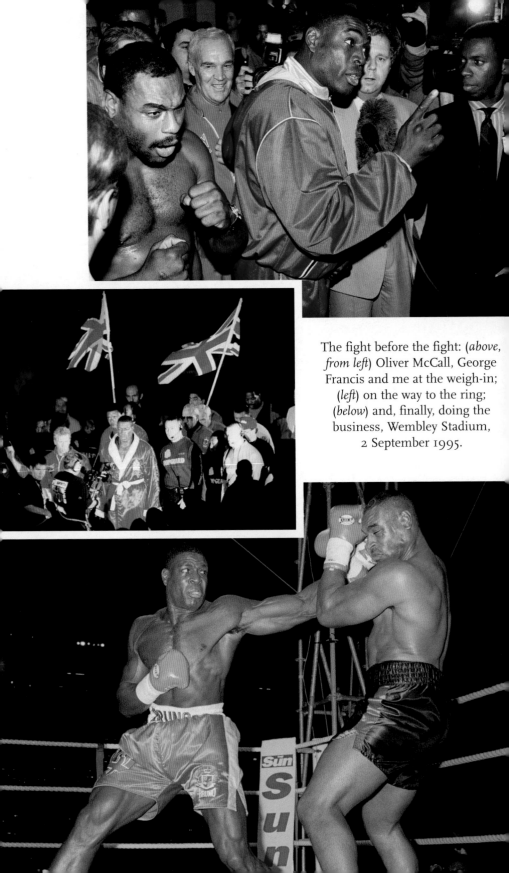

The fight before the fight: (*above, from left*) Oliver McCall, George Francis and me at the weigh-in; (*left*) on the way to the ring; (*below*) and, finally, doing the business, Wembley Stadium, 2 September 1995.

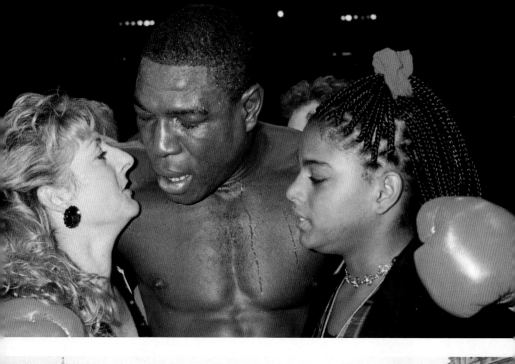

p) The happiest night of my life: Laura and Nicola
·lebrate the world title. (*Above*) And then so do the
rest of London...

(*Right*) Me with Franklin Jr, 1995.

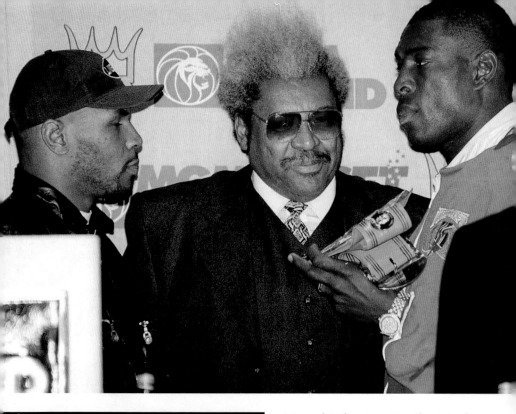

Me and Mike, Part II. (*Above*) At the press conference with Tyson and Don King – Laura's cheering me on (*left*). (*Below*) The last walk: I'd felt so good about the fight beforehand; now it was all going wrong. (*Opposite*) The final seconds of my career, MGM Grand, 16 March 1996.

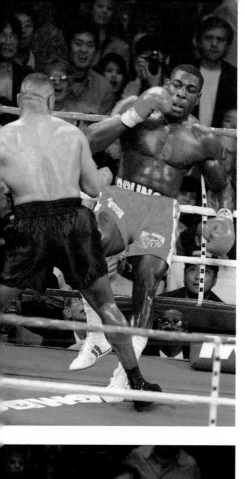

Good times: DJing with my nephews
(*left to right*) Trevor Rowe, Nigel Hamilton
and Andrew Nesbeth.

Bad times: September 2003 – days before
my breakdown, and it's just me and Sooty

A break in the storm: the photographers were never far away –
even when I left hospital for a brief trip home.

Y106 KNO

My family: they mean the world to me – at the Dorchester, London, 2005.

Better days: June 2005 – with Russell Crowe at Ricky Hatton's title fight; and opening the Bellingdon and Asheridge fête in July.

Frank Bruno, fighting back – then and now.

born in London. I've lived here all my life. In my opinion, Lennox was using the flag because he knew it would make him more money. I may never have had the chance to fight for the British title, which I regret, but I've always been proud of my country. The way I saw it, Lewis was trying to paint a picture of me as a stooge, someone who was being used. I was nobody's stooge. I was in the fight game and I was doing what I had to do to get where I wanted to go. I was using boxing as much as boxing was using me. I was in the using business. Just like he was.

I don't have a problem with people coming to live here. How could I? My mother and father came here from the West Indies. I'm proud of those roots too. But I don't have to go shouting about it. And I don't use my heritage to have a go at another black man. I think it was Lennox who had the identity problem. I was comfortable being a black Briton.

I respect what Lennox has done and acknowledge that he became a fine champion. But some wounds are harder to heal than others. I don't hold a grudge any more. It's not in my nature. Let's just say I've moved on from that episode. We settled our argument and, as far as I'm concerned, that's that. We've met since and there is no animosity any more. But at the time I was as angry as I'd ever been.

'What he's saying about you is disgraceful,' George said, when he heard the reports. 'But you've got to try to ignore it. Don't let it get to you.'

But you can imagine the rage that was building up inside me. I couldn't wait to get him in the ring but I had to stay cool. If I lost my head, he'd slaughter me, because he is a seriously good boxer. So was I, though. I might not have been Muhammad Ali or Joe Louis. I never pretended to be. But I improved as my career went on. I worked hard on my skills. My defence tightened up and I added combinations to the big one-punch hitting of my early days. I could put together uppercuts and hooks, I could hook off my jab and I always had a wicked right cross, long or short. I think those are tools any heavyweight would be proud of. And I was never less than 100 per cent fit. For the Lewis fight, I trained the house down.

Laura was as tense as I was before the fight. She'd swapped words with Frank Maloney, Lewis's manager, and was in no mood to be messed about. There was so much emotion building up in me, I knew I was going to perform like never before.

I wanted the fight at Wembley, my second home. But, for various reasons, we ended up at the old Cardiff Arms Park. I didn't mind that much. I liked the Welsh and they seemed to like me. But it was some risk putting it on outdoors at that time of year. It can get pretty wet in Wales in October. They even wrote a rain clause into the rules. If rain stopped the fight after four rounds, whoever was leading on points would win the title. We were right to be worried. The rains held off most of the evening but, as it was going out at 1 a.m. for American television, it was inevitable we'd get caught sooner or later.

When it came, it wasn't that heavy but it was enough to make things difficult. There was a big canopy over the ring in the middle of the rugby pitch, and they put down a new canvas after the undercard fights. I even wore plastic over my boots on the walk to the ring so the soles wouldn't get wet. These were all distractions. But after everything I'd been through, I hardly noticed.

I know his jab is fast and hard. I know he's got a long reach. So I have to concentrate on staying under it or wide of it. I don't want to give him a launching pad for his right cross, the punch he landed on Razor Ruddock's jaw.

I take the first round. I'm outboxing him, simple as that. I feint with my jab, then bring my right cross over. It confuses him. I don't think he reckons I have much of a boxing brain. How wrong can he be? George and I have been working on these variations for weeks. I'm boxing like I've never boxed before.

Round two. More of the same. I've got an answer for every-thing Lewis tries. I push him back with my strength and go to work with my combinations.

Round three. I'm feeling great. Getting stronger. I know I'm hurting Lewis. I feel it every time my punches connect. And I see it in his eyes. He's shocked. He realises I'm for real. He knows I'm no phoney, no stooge. He knows he's in the toughest fight of his life, and it's in front of a British audience. I can hear the drenched crowd around the Arms Park, and not much of it's for Lennox. The noise carries only one word through the night: 'Broo-no!' Over and over again. It's the sweetest sound. Sweeter than my mother's singing in church.

Round four. Lewis gets his boxing together. He's back in the fight. 'Concentrate, Frank, concentrate,' George had said at the end of the third. I'm concentrating like a rocket scientist. I'm looking out for that right hand because, when it comes, it's got pain written all over it. Strangely, he keeps it in his locker. Maybe he's the one who's not concentrating.

Round five. Still feel good. The jab, the uppercut, the hook. They're all working smoothly. I'm doing a number on Lennox and I can tell he doesn't like it. I must be in front.

Round six. I'm in a zone. The punches are flowing smooth as hot honey. Lewis can't get out of the way of my jab and I know he's tiring. I hear it in his breathing. Nothing he tries works. Everything I put together gets home. I can't miss him.

Round seven. Maybe I can end it now. I back Lewis up on the ropes. All the pain, all the insults – he's paying for it now. He shouldn't have said those things. He should have had respect. That right hand, that's for what you said, man. That left, that's for dissing me to my people. The crowd is going crazy again. The roar is immense. He's there for the taking. And he knows it. 'One more punch, Frank!' I hear George yell from the corner. 'One more! You've got him!' And then . . . Lewis steps on my foot, I look away for an instant, we tangle up, I expect the referee to break us apart. He does. But Lennox is back on me in a second, just as I relax. He lands – not the right, but the left hook. It's a devastating punch – I know that the second it rattles my jaw. I reel away, back against the ropes. He's on me now. The little I do see is red and leather and it's coming at me at a hundred miles an hour. One punch after another. Maybe twenty in all. They nearly all land. I can't stop the storm. And I don't think to hang on. I want to fight. Just like I did against Bonecrusher. Just like I did against Witherspoon. Just like I did against Tyson. That's the way I'm made. I don't want to hang on. I want to hit back. But there's no time, no space. No way. Lennox is ruthless. He sets about finishing the job. Still, he can't put me down. Punch after punch crashes into my head. He puts a glove on my neck, sizes me up and lets another piledriver go. I'm still standing. I don't know how. And then I see the towel again, the white flag. George has seen enough. It's over. Again . . .

Afterwards, the atmosphere was as nasty as it had been before the fight. The press conference was loud and angry. For me, it was an argument that hadn't been settled. But I had only myself to blame. I looked away for a second, I got nailed. George was shattered. Laura was still wound up, still furious with Frank Maloney. I was confused and devastated. Could I come back from this? Would they give me another chance? Did I still want it?

My mother didn't. She begged me to quit. I could understand it. She'd never liked me fighting. She reckoned I'd earned enough to walk away. And she was right. But I would be walking away a loser. And no amount of money could buy back my dignity if I left now. I'm a proud man. Sometimes pride gets in the way of making the right decision, but there was nothing I could do about it. In my soul, I knew what I had to do. Not many believed in me now, even though I'd put in the performance of my life. I can't think of a single writer who wanted me to carry on. That didn't matter much to me. They were entitled to their

173

opinions. I knew I had more in me. And I wasn't kidding myself.

'Mickey,' I said, 'get me another fight as soon as you can. I'm going to prove the lot of them wrong. Trust me.'

He did what he does best, lined me up with an American I could beat up to get myself back into contention. I didn't care. I just wanted one more shot. If I had to fight no-hopers to get there, I'd do it.

Five months later I put away a guy called Jessie 'Boogieman' Ferguson. It was nearly as embarrassing as the Chuck Gardner fiasco. He was thirty-six, fat and obliging. Although he'd been in a world title fight a year earlier, it had been a two-round farce against Riddick Bowe. I was all over the place, banging him around the back of the neck. It was extremely ugly. And short. Just under three minutes.

I took a break. And said goodbye to Mickey. We'd been together fourteen years and, mostly, they'd been good ones. But it was time to move on – and the man I turned to was Frank Warren. He was Mickey's biggest rival and had a contract with Sky. My first fight for him was in February '95. It was an unlikely setting: Shepton Mallet, a market town in Somerset. Most of us had never heard of it. Certainly, Rodolfo Marin won't remember it with any fondness. The Puerto Rican entered the ring with a big kneepad on. Just as well. He fell to the canvas from my first serious punch, a long right hand. I put him down again with a left and he decided he'd had enough. It was awful.

So was Mike Evans. He said he'd beaten Mike Tyson as an amateur. I reckon it must have been with a baseball bat when Tyson wasn't looking. That one was in the Kelvin Hall in Glasgow in May. It lasted two rounds. You don't really need to know more than that about the evening – except that it was on Sky and, amazingly, that the win put me in line to challenge for the world title again. What a weird and wonderful business I was in.

14

'I Thank God I Won'

'LADIES AND GENTLEMEN. AFTER TWELVE ROUNDS OF BOXING we
have a unanimous decision . . . The winner and *new* . . .'

The night I beat Oliver McCall I put behind me all the
disappointments. The defeats, the pain, the arguments, the
sacrifices – none of that mattered any more. It felt so good
I can hardly bear thinking about it. I even hugged Don King.
Jimmy Lennon Jr never got to finish his announcement.
People piled into the ring from everywhere. Laura rushed
into my arms. We hadn't seen each other for seven weeks
and she was kissing me before they'd had a chance to wipe
the blood from my mouth. I lost it completely. Millions of
people saw the heavyweight champion of the world break
down in tears. I didn't care.

I was sitting on the edge of the ring, my face covered in
blood, sweat and tears. The TV mike was right in my face and
I just let rip. 'I thank God I won . . . I'm not an Uncle Tom,
I'm not an Uncle Tom, I'm not a sell-out.' I'd proved everyone

wrong, the critics, the doubters, the trash talkers, the people who said I was washed up – and Oliver McCall. Lennox Lewis had tried it on. So did McCall. And he paid for it.

Getting a world title shot requires more than boxing ability. I should know: I'd had three. After losing to Lewis, I wasn't sure I'd be given another chance. I was thirty-three and there were a lot of other hungry fighters out there. You have to wonder if you're still box office, whether you've still got the fire in your belly.

Frank Warren had been a rival promoter most of my career. But he pulled out all the stops to get me a title shot. Getting McCall meant going through Don King. Again.

Some fighters said they didn't like to work with King. But sooner or later, most of them did. Fighters will go with whoever gets them good money. Slim Robinson, an old trainer who used to work with King fighters, once said you might earn a million dollars and King would earn six million, but that would be a million you never would have earned otherwise. That's just the way it is, man.

Don's strategy was simple: you did the deal with him, or there was no deal. He didn't give you any other options. To get the fight with McCall – even though I'd earned the right to be considered a legitimate challenger – I had to let Don choose my next opponent. There was nothing else on the table. The money was fine, it could have done with a couple of extra noughts here and there, but I didn't have too many complaints on that front. It was just that Don laid down the law and I had to fall into line.

When we did the deal at the Grosvenor House Hotel in

the spring of '95, they wouldn't let my lawyer into the room. I wish they had. It was just the four of us: Don, Frank, me and Laura. King came in, loud as you like, and threw the contract down in front of us.

'Take it or leave it,' he said. Some negotiation. There was nothing I could say. It wasn't a mandatory defence. McCall could fight whoever he wanted to. I had to pay a price. A big one. If I won, my first defence would be against Mike Tyson.

I got the impression they thought Oliver would win easily. Lennox Lewis had stopped me in 1993. A year later, McCall knocked Lewis out in the first round. That's how he got the title. They called Oliver the 'Atomic Bull' – and he lived up to it. But you tell someone they've got no chance and, if they've got any bottle, it will fire them up. It worked for me. They were messing me about with the deal. They had given me no respect.

There would be more drama. There was a bit of history to this one, and it started at the Docklands Arena in London a month before we signed the deal. Nigel Benn's fight with Gerald McClellan was one of the most emotional experiences any of us could remember. Poor Gerald was carried from the ring with serious brain damage. He's now blind and in a wheelchair. It was one of those nights all fighters dread. Including Nigel.

There had been all sorts of bad vibes before and after that fight, but I put it down to hype. I know Nigel did. Afterwards, though, when Gerald was lying in hospital, his family and Nigel really went to it in the papers. It was nasty. It was as if they thought Nigel meant to put Gerald in hospital, that he was glad about what had happened. He wasn't at all. I know he was really upset about it. But it's the risk we run.

And then the Atomic Bull came to town. I knew Oliver. He'd been my sparring partner when I was training for the Tyson fight in '89, and I liked him. But he comes from a bad-mouthing background, where gutter language is common. Oliver charged right in as soon as he got near a microphone. I had the feeling this was going to be no ordinary press conference. Almost the first thing he did was to call me an Uncle Tom. I'd been through this with Lennox. I wasn't going to stand for it again. Then McCall made as cheap a shot as I can remember one fighter making about another. 'I'm going to do to you what Benn did to McClellan. I'm here for vengeance.' He said he was going to turn me into a vegetable.

I just stared at him. I could hardly believe what he'd said. King was sitting next to him, and he looked to me to see how I'd react. A full-scale row wouldn't hurt ticket sales, but I didn't want to know about either of these two guys. Even when McCall started having a go at Laura too. That was really out of order. He went on about me marrying a white girl and how I had turned my back on 'the brothers'. It was all such a nonsense, and I wondered if he'd been coached. I didn't think Oliver would've come up with this stuff himself.

I blanked them all. My mind was totally on the fight. I went back to the gym, a health farm in Leicestershire, and took it out on my sparring partners. I wasn't going to blow my fourth chance. I wasn't going to repeat my earlier mistakes. Against Witherspoon, Tyson and Lewis, one way

or another, I'd let the occasion get to me. I had to get everything right this time.

Tearing into McCall was not the way to win the title. I had
to be in total control of myself. I had to fight my fight, a
measured, disciplined fight that would frustrate the champion. Oliver was a very emotional man. He just put himself
in top gear and went for it. I would be cleverer than that. I
was going to make him pay for the things he said.

I reckoned I knew more about McCall than McCall knew
about me. When we sparred six years before, he was an
absolute sucker for my jab. He just put his face in front of
it. Not once did he try to slip the punch. Maybe he thought
that's what he was getting paid for. But he had one hell of a
chin. So I knew he'd be no pushover.

I put that information in the bank and worked on a few
other tricks. George, astute as ever, had me avoiding the sort
of cracking right McCall used on Lewis. Every time my sparring partners would go to throw a right, I would move to my
right to nullify it, with my left hand high. And Oliver's right
was one serious weapon . . .

When it comes to the real showdown, in the ring, McCall is still
playing his mind games. But I'm not sure he's totally in control
of himself. I'm the challenger, so I've entered the ring first. And
the reception is just as I knew it would be, loud enough to be
heard five miles away. But where's the champ? He takes fifteen
minutes to get into the ring. Maybe he's trying to make me fret.
Maybe he's the one having an anxiety attack. I look at George,
who seems more wound up than I do. We don't say much. We
never did. I'm in control, revved up with the handbrake on.

When McCall finally makes it through the ropes he looks as if he's just been given some horrible news. I wonder if he knows I've already signed to fight Tyson if I win tonight. He might have found out. You don't want to be told your opponent is being lined up for his next fight before he's even got this one out the way. Oliver has had personal problems. He's had a crack habit on and off since he was a teenager. He's also been in trouble with the law. He could be a time bomb. Now he does something remarkable. As he looks across the ring at me he starts crying. Not like he's been hurt but as if he's suffering inside his head. It all looks too much for him. He's sweating up hugely and his eyes are bulging. It's obvious he's not under control. This could be dangerous. If he doesn't know what he's doing, it will make my job harder. Will he go berserk?

The music is filling the stadium, but I hear him shout across the ring, 'You've got no chance, Bruno. You're out of here.' Behind him are his hangers-on, screaming their heads off. It's motherfucker this and motherfucker that. He's brought nearly thirty people with him, all sponging as hard as they can. Everything's on Oliver's tab. They've got flight tickets and hotel rooms. And no manners. I've never had that many people around me. Friends don't want to be part of that circus. Not if they're real friends.

My little crew is George, Keith Morton, who looks after my fitness, John Bloomfield, who works the corner with George, my masseur Rupert Doaries and my brother Michael. That's plenty. The rest of my friends are at ringside. And the loudest of all of them is Nigel Benn. He's been on the under-card tonight; he stopped a guy called Danny Perez to keep his world title. He still found time to get changed and lead me to the ring, carrying the Union Jack. Like me, he's proud to be British. I'm well pleased to have his big grinning face here. I did the same for him when he fought McClellan. He's never said he was a saint – but he's always been a good friend to me.

Now, not far from my corner there's a man in a wheel-chair. He's a pretty special guy too. Four years ago, he fought Chris Eubank at White Hart Lane. Michael Watson has never fallen out of love with boxing, which is a shock to some people. Weird? I don't think so. It's in his blood.

Seeing him at ringside makes me stronger. It makes me realise we have to overcome all sorts of setbacks. If you run away from them you'll never know what you could have achieved. I've never ducked a challenge in my life. Michael has overcome. I've overcome. And we both will again.

King is sitting to my left. I'm not so thrilled to see him. He starts cackling, like he does whenever the heat goes up. Putting on a big fight gives him a rush. He loves to see how much power he has over people. He looks around Wembley. He knows he's pulled it off again. You have to hand it to him, he's the best in the business at selling tickets.

It's always a relief to hear the first bell. There's no turning back now. No walking away. I put my big jab on McCall as soon as I get him in range. Just like when we sparred. I can tell he doesn't fancy it. He's taking it, but he isn't in love with it. There isn't much coming back. That's a surprise. His corner start up with their mad shouting. 'Give it to him, champ! Make him pay!' Outside the ring I've got at least 20,000 in my corner. No contest. I land with a sweet left, flush on that rocklike jaw. McCall judders like a mountain that's had a stick of dynamite explode on it. He wobbles, then just as quickly recovers. That's some chin.

Towards the end of the first round. I take a stinging blow, not that heavy, but bang on my right eyeball. Something's not right. McCall's glove has collided with my eye in just the wrong place. It's scratched the surface. I'm in agony. But I can't let on. Any show of weakness and McCall will be all over me. My eye is weeping. I mustn't blink. There could be half an hour of this to go. I'll have to dig deep to get through it. Am I going to fail again? I don't want to even think about it.

George wipes my face at the end of the round and says, 'Well done, Frank.' Then he sees it. He sees the blinking. 'What's up with the eye, Frank?'

'Don't worry, George. Nothing. I'm fine.'

He knows I'm lying, but this is no time for lengthy discussions. If it gets worse, George will spot it. For now he doesn't want to disturb my rhythm. Nor do I.

I have to stay calm. I have to remember everything George and I have talked about. The punch I'm holding back is my right cross. I don't want to telegraph it. I know McCall's waiting for it. That's how he beat Lewis; they both unloaded at the same time but Oliver's right got home a fraction of a second first. He's no fancy dan boxer but he knows the basics. If he sees a gap, he'll throw the right as hard as he can. Simple as that.

He stays on the move. I'm waiting for him to explode. His cornermen are still going over the top. I keep pumping out the jab and it's getting home. Any time he looks like coming to life, I tie him up. It's what I'd tried to do against Tyson.

'Keep that up, Frank,' George says at the end of the second. Why wouldn't I? I know everyone in the country wants a knockout – but what I want is the title. I know the crowd mean well but they aren't throwing the punches. Or taking them. Oliver is still dangerous. But I've started so well I can practically taste victory.

I put in the occasional right. I'm hurting him, I can feel it. But he's taking his beating well. Oliver is one of the toughest men who ever got in a boxing ring. Or maybe one of the toughest men ever. I'm boxing at my absolute peak. I can't miss him, even with one bad eye.

George reckons it couldn't be better. But we thought that when I fought Bonecrusher, and the night Witherspoon came from behind, and Lewis . . . I've learnt my lessons. I'm not going to roar in and try to finish it, whatever the growing noise behind me. 'Broo-no! Broo-no!' They're getting their money's worth, by the sound of it.

It's the fourth. I land another perfect left hook and McCall is in trouble. For a split second I think about jumping on him to finish it. With just about anyone else, I would have done. Not tonight. His head clears and I stick with my game plan. Out goes the jab.

George reckons I need to slow down a little. He doesn't want me blowing up later on, and he's right. McCall hasn't noticed I'm struggling with my eye. He hasn't had the chance. I've been all over him. Going into the fifth, I can sense he's losing his rag. We clinch. Neither of us wants to let go; we're fighting for breath. Then he comes to life, finally. A couple of his jabs get through, but the tape on my left glove unravels and George takes as long as he can to put it back on. At the end, I take a big left. Now we've got a fight.

George is worried I might get too involved but I know I won't. I've done most of the work so far and must have a decent points lead, but I've still got seven rounds to go. And I've got a dodgy eye. George has cottoned on to that by now but he doesn't want to dwell on it. He knows I've got to concentrate on the job. We'll worry about the eye later. I know McCall will be as strong in the second half of the fight as in the first. All I've got to do is more of the same.

I'm right to be cautious. In the sixth I can feel McCall getting back into the fight. George is on my case. 'Keep working, Frank, don't let him back into the fight. You're doing fine.' We're coming up to the seventh, the round Lewis stopped me. My eye is still bothering me, but I'm trying to ignore it. I have to come through this, keep going – all the way to the finish line. It'll be worth it. Just over twenty minutes and I'll be champion of the world.

McCall backs me up and I catch him with a chop to the back of the neck. The referee, Tony Perez, warns me to cut it out. Nigel Benn has other ideas. 'Keep that up, Frank!' he shouts at me. So much advice. Anyway, I'm cool. We go back at it, with a couple of big exchanges. It's toe to toe now and I'm in with a bit of a monster. But so is he.

I'm pleased with my boxing. I'm in control. I know I've taken his boxing away from him, I just have to watch out for the big right hand. But I've thrown so many lefts my arm is getting heavier by the minute. I switch to lead with my right. McCall senses something is up and throws himself at me. I hold him off and get through to the end of the eighth in reasonable shape.

McCall steps on the accelerator. He knows he needs a knockout to win. But I've got my jab going again in the ninth. I start to tire in the tenth and McCall gives me everything he's got, to head and body. My legs are so heavy, my eye is blinking madly now. I struggle for air. He catches me with an almighty uppercut. But I wrap myself in his arms.

Two to go. Only six minutes. Seems like an hour. Will I make it? Hard to concentrate. 'Come on, Frank!' screams George. It's as if I'm in a tunnel. I ache in the ribs and face. My eyeball is suffering. My good eye is hurting too. 'Don't throw it away now, Frank!' George shouts in my ear. McCall charges at me. This, the eleventh, is his best round. He's winging hooks at me. He's not worried about lining me up for an opening. He's just slinging them, like a drunk outside a pub. I catch him with a decent right-hand counter, then a right uppercut. He holds. I hold. He motions to the referee that I'm making it hard for him to let his punches go. And he's right. The referee, much smaller than either of us, prises us apart. I am glad to get to the end of the round.

Only three minutes to go. 'You're way in front, Frank,' says George. 'This is everything you've wanted. I know you won't blow it. It's about surviving. Get to the finish, Frank, and the world title is yours. Three minutes, Frank. Three minutes.' Time, suddenly, is the most important thing in my life. Every second is stretched. It is like I'm going through life in super-slow motion. McCall carries the fight to me again. Unbelievably, he seems to be getting stronger.

Where does he get it from? You could hit him all night with a sledgehammer and he'd still be standing.

He's the one doing the hitting, now. And he's really loading up. I have my gloves around my head, and he works the body. I drop my arms to protect my ribs, and he goes back upstairs, throwing those hooks around my shoulders and head. Enough get through. I'm prepared to give up this round to him because I trust George's judgement. I know I'm well ahead. It's the final half-minute. Even McCall is gasping for air. He has me on the ropes again, belting away, anywhere. I reckon we're nearly through . . . Then we are. That blessed bell goes. I feel the most tremendous release. The place goes wild. I turn to George, good old George. Not sure if he's crying. I've only got one good eye, after all.

The usual madness follows. I'm the Guv'nor. Number 1.

The crowd's gone now. Drunk and happy. We're off home soon. Just the urine sample for the drugs test left. Someone says McCall hasn't given his B sample. What's up there, then? I wonder. No matter. It's all done. There's talk of a big party. But that's not my scene. George isn't keen either. We don't bother. All that work, the drama, the excitement . . . and home to a cup of tea.

The morning after I got a knock on the door and there were my two best supporters in boxing, Nigel Benn and Michael Watson. I don't normally go over my fights but this was special. We went through every punch, from start to finish. It was great talking business with two guys who had been there – two guys who had fought each other as well. It's what makes boxing special. I know a lot of athletes swap old stories after their careers are over, but with boxers the tales are different. They are about another level of sport – about life and death. We risk everything each time we get in the ring.

I'd joined a special club. Over the last century or so, only forty heavyweights have been universally recognised as the best fighting man in the world. Think about that. There is nothing to match it in sport. You're on top of the mountain looking down at every single fighter in the business. And you know you're the best.

I would be champion for a mere six months. And, unknown to anyone but myself and my trainer, I would go into the Tyson fight with one good eye.

15
Tyson II

THE VERY NICEST SECOND OF THE VERY BEST MINUTE OF THE FINEST hour of my life was when the referee held my hand up to say I was the heavyweight champion of the world. The high should have lasted a long time – not just that night and the weeks that followed. Wicked. But, you know what? From the moment I became champion, it could only be downhill. From that very second. It could never be that good again. And it never was. I'm not saying it was bad. How could it be? But I wouldn't feel that natural high again. And, when I think about it now, that great, unbelievable, unrepeatable feeling lasted maybe a minute.

I'm not sure how long it took me to come back down to earth. I was buzzing like a bee that night. So was Oliver. But then he was always an excitable boy.

I knew I couldn't get carried away with the romance of being the undisputed world champion. It's a fancy belt. But it's also a way to make money. Those are the facts. If it was just the title, with no money, it would be an Olympic gold medal or some other trophy. And I'm not knocking that. What a thrill it must be to win a medal for your country. But I'm just telling you the way it is in professional boxing. It's not a fairy tale. What's real in boxing is the power at the end of your arm and the clout you have when you walk into your bank. If you land your shot on the other guy's chin and he goes down and doesn't get up – tell me, what's more real than that?

But the satisfaction I got from beating McCall wasn't just about the money, or revenge for what he said, or the romance of it all. It was about my standing in the fight game. It was about respect. Nobody was going to say I was chinny, call me a clown. I wasn't Frank Bruno the panto star, I wasn't the HP Sauce man, and I definitely wasn't an Uncle Tom. I was the man who beat the man who beat the man who beat the man, all the way back through a hundred years or so. All the way back to Bob Fitzsimmons. And Jack Dempsey and Joe Louis. All those great names. I could put mine along-side theirs. That's something. I'm not saying I'm as good as they were. But I did what they did. I did what I had to do. And then I met Tyson again.

So much had happened to Mike since February '89. For years, he had been suffering in his own way. They were the sort of troubles that still lay ahead of me, although of course I didn't know it at the time. And, like me, he had to do it in public. You don't expect too much privacy when you're famous; you do expect a little humanity. His first wife had left him, he'd lost the people who'd cared for him and he'd lost his world title. His life had fallen apart.

Then, in March 1992, he was sentenced to six years in jail

for raping a beauty queen called Desiree Washington. He behaved and got out after three years.

In 1995 Mike was back among us as the man the world loved to hate. I'm not saying he didn't deserve it – he'd done some terrible things – but it was weird. People loathed him, but they couldn't look away. If anything he was bigger box office than before. It was only a matter of time before he lost it completely, and everyone wanted to see the car crash on prime-time TV.

He hooked up with Don King again, and had two fights in 1995. Well, Don called them fights, but they were more like trips to the cash machine. Mike got $25 million for ninety seconds' work against Peter McNeeley and $10 million for watching Buster Mathis Jr fall over in front of him.

I wondered if he'd put his life back together again. You never knew with Mike. For a smart guy, he's done so many dumb things. He's good at mind games, he's a clever boxer, but he doesn't always get it right in real life. Certainly he got confused. He had a cheerleader called 'the Crocodile', a pair of managers, John Horne and Rory Holloway, who were friends of Don King's, and a million other hangers-on. Later, when he was used up, they'd all be gone. But in 1996 they were still on the scene.

Mike was spending money at an amazing rate. He could shop for America. He celebrated getting out of jail by buying ten Rolls-Royces, ten BMWs, a couple of Bentleys and a couple of mansions. He obviously needed the parking space. They reckon that between 1995 and 1997 he earned $122 million. And spent $115 million. He must have figured there'd always be plenty on tap.

It was the golden rule of boxing: if you fought Mike, you made money. Good money. The trick for most fighters was holding on to it. I'd been lucky to have good people around me all my career, so I wasn't exactly skint. I knew it was my last fight – this was my pension. I wanted a big pay day, one that would set me, Laura and the kids up for the rest of our lives. It was nowhere near what I was after – but that wasn't my idea. In fact, the fight wasn't my idea in the first place.

Nothing felt right. Fourteen years – almost to the day – since my first professional fight, I was finishing my career in Las Vegas, the mecca of boxing. But this was no happy anniversary, no sentimental goodbye to the ring. It wasn't supposed to be like this. The wonderful, indescribable feeling I'd had six months earlier at Wembley had gone. It had been replaced by an emptiness I tried to ignore.

I'd been working hard at the World Gym for weeks. Normally I loved training. There was even a Tyson lookalike among my sparring partners, a guy called Cliff Couser. You can imagine I didn't go lightly on him. But it just wasn't doing it for me. I felt uneasy. 'The Crocodile' and other members of Tyson's posse were in my face – literally. They'd even be there when I went out running at dawn. The mood was more aggressive than normal. The press conferences were hell. There was screaming and shouting every day. It never stopped. King was doing his thing, trying to mess with my mind. And, all the time, I knew I shouldn't even have been there.

Tyson was doing OK. He had the best suite at the MGM, the red carpet treatment all the way. He was getting

$30 million, even though he was the challenger. I was getting $6 million. The champion normally gets the bigger cut. Really, I should have had about $21 million. It seemed like everyone wanted Tyson to win. It was doing my head in.

Only a few people know what it's like to be mucked about like this. Boxers put up with it all the time. We only ask for what we're worth – and they call us greedy. But you don't get many chances to make big money in the fight game. When you do, you have to bargain as hard as you can. Negotiating with King drained me, and it drained Laura. There were arguments you wouldn't believe. Don wasn't just in show business. He was in the Don King business, the Make-Don-King-Even-Richer business.

There was also the small matter of my eye. It was the reason this was going to be my last fight. And only George and I knew the whole story. George was the best friend I had in the business – aside from Laura. I trusted him completely. And if he trusted you, there was nothing he wouldn't do for you. Just as well. I was about to ask him for a hell of a favour.

When McCall landed that punch on my right eyeball I knew something was wrong straight away. It wouldn't stop flickering. It went on for days, weeks, months. Even when we got to Vegas, it was still giving me grief. I knew something was wrong, but I didn't want to see a doctor. I didn't want anyone telling me my career was already over. I knew the truth – I just wanted to postpone it for one more fight.

Meanwhile, I had to pass a medical. I decided to wing it.

'We're going to have to be a bit clever here, Frank,' George said, on our way to the Nevada State Athletic Commission. 'Leave it to me.' George had performed a few miracles in the past – but how was he going to convince them I didn't have a dodgy eye?

I knew the Commission's doctors would be impressed. They'd seen me before. I was a dedicated trainer, my heart and lungs were working fine. My brain scans were good too. Then came the moment I'd been dreading. Time to look at my eyes.

George went to work. I'm still not sure how he pulled it off. He started jabbering on to the doctor about something or other. On and on, distracting him from his examination. I kept shtum. George was making ridiculous small talk. Might have been the weather. Or the casinos. Anything but boxing. Anyway, it worked. The doctor took a look and passed me fit to fight. He never stood a chance with all of George's blarney.

I got up, shook the doctor's hand and thanked him for his time. I couldn't believe we'd got away with it. It was wrong, certainly. But what else could I do? I knew it was my last fight anyway.

Now I'd passed my MOT. Nothing left to do but wait for the night, the last night of my career. And I was taking into the ring a very dangerous secret.

In the dressing room at the MGM, a quarter of an hour before the fight. Frank Warren's there. So's Laura, my brother Michael and a few others. I feel good. My body's ready. I've trained well. George is running a hand over my shoulders, keeping my muscles loose. I try to stop my right eye blinking.

I look around the room. Everyone seems upbeat. 'You can do this, Frank,' says Frank Warren. 'This is your time. You're the champion, you're the man.'

Then something strange happens. There's a knock at the door. A guy pokes his head in: 'Five minutes. Get ready for the ring walk.'

I can't explain it but something goes pop in my head. The energy drains from my body. I feel empty and alone. It's not fear. I'm used to handling that. I've been a fighter for so long I know fear will arrive before a fight. Usually I turn it away. This is something else. I've lost my peace of mind. I can't block out the worries and doubts and anger. Everything that's gone wrong over the past few months fills my head. The belief I'd had only a few moments ago is slipping away.

I just want to get in the ring. Get it over with. The longer I sit here the worse it gets. I look up and see Frank Warren's face. He's worried. I look at George. He probably senses it too, but he hides it well. He always did.

'Let's go, Frank,' he says. 'Let's get this done.'

I can't get out of the dressing room fast enough. The ring is where the world becomes real again.

As we enter the arena, the noise starts. 'Broo-no! Broo-no!' I've heard it all my career. From the Albert Hall to the MGM. It's part of my soul. But it's different tonight. I'll never hear it again, not as a fighter. This *is* my farewell, and only George and I know it.

I enter the ring sweating and crossing myself – seventeen times, some people say. The TV people will play that shot again and again. They'll say I'm scared shitless. It's not that simple. Deep down, I'm not happy about being here. I don't feel like a champion. How can I be the real champion if the bookies have me at 10–1? I should feel brilliant. I feel sick.

I've never had a rematch before. Except with Joe Christle.

That was so long ago. I came through that, but God I was worried before it. This is Tyson. I have one hope: get to the centre of the ring and keep him on the end of my jab. If I use my power, if I connect properly, he will go. But I have to be careful. Not get tagged early like I did last time. No getting in close, no getting caught on the ropes. Have to stay away from the hooks, tie him up, push him off, jab, look for an opening. I've got to nail him. And hope he doesn't notice my flickering right eye.

Round one. Tyson takes the short route across the ring. I chop him with a couple of stiff shots. I feel good. But he's swinging hard. He's sharp. You'd never know he'd been away. I'm in for a tough night.

I'm looking for one good shot. One good shot will steady him. It'll keep him off, give me time to size him up. But I can't get set. It's like the first fight. He's all over me. He hardly misses. It's a bad round. He's opened a cut over my good eye. That's all I need.

Round two. Mike's gone up a gear. How's that possible? All I can do is hang on. Mills Lane, the referee, takes a point off me. It hardly matters. This is not going to points. I've got to remember what George always says. Do whatever it takes to get back into the fight. I'm thinking straight, but I'm not making any headway. Tyson's buzzing. He's hurling everything into my arms and head, around my elbows and into my ribs.

Round three. God, he's quick. I've hardly got out of my corner. I'm back against the ropes. The head shots are getting through. That's one, two, three . . . I soak them up. As best I can. Six, seven, eight . . . The strength's leaving my legs . . . Nine, ten, eleven . . . Another enormous belt to the side of my head. I slide to the bottom rope. Lane has seen enough. The end.

I look up at Tyson. It's an awful feeling. I never got into the fight. I didn't hit him with a single good shot. He puts his arm around me, then he gets the WBC belt around his waist. My belt.

Back in the dressing room I take a shower and wash the blood from my face. I ache everywhere but mostly inside. The *Sun* have been on the phone to Laura. We've done another good deal selling my few words to them. Business as usual. But not for much longer . . .

They say most fighters go out with a loss. That doesn't make it any easier. I'd had a picture in my head. It was the same picture I'd had for seven years. Tyson comes at me like a lion, I steady him with a jab. I hold him off, wear him down . . . and knock him out. For ten years Tyson had been the man every heavyweight wanted. The man we all measured ourselves against. I knew I could have beaten him, proved I was the best. Who knows, maybe if I'd met him back in '88, when we were first meant to fight, things would have been different. I'd never know.

I should have been relieved it was all over, I guess. No more monkey business. No more arguments with promoters and managers. No more hassles, a chance to chill out at last, to enjoy life. Yes, that would be good. Back to Essex to put my feet up. I had plenty of money in the bank, a loving wife and two beautiful kids. Another on the way. Surely I couldn't want more than that?

Losing to Tyson a second time wasn't just about coping with defeat. The pain I felt the night boxing had finally done with me and I had done with boxing went far deeper. I'd come to learn that I could never replace what had been the central part of my life, from the moment I woke up until I went to sleep, every day of every week of every year.

George and I had one last chat about the whole business. We'd been together for nearly ten years and we knew there'd be no more nights like this, good or bad. He didn't want to train anyone else. He was going to pack it in too.

'So, Frank,' he said, as he put his big arm around my shoulder, 'what have you got in mind?'

'Don't know, George . . . Go home and count the chandeliers?'

16

Drugs, Divorce and Depression

THE CHANDELIERS AT STONDON MASSEY WERE NICE ENOUGH. SO was the rest of the house. The acres of land. The gadgets. The cars. These were the things my fists had earned me down the years. This is what I wanted. Wasn't it?

I still worked out. As a big man, I knew I could go to fat, and I like to keep in shape. So I stuck to near enough the same regime I had when I was boxing. Going for a run. Hundreds of sit-ups. A few light weights. A bit of skipping. I had no need for gloves. There was nobody to spar with. What was the point of sparring anyway? I wasn't a fighter any more. I was . . . well, I wasn't sure what I was. I was an ex-boxer with a dodgy eye. I was thirty-five years old and I didn't have a job. Sure, I had money. Millions. I had a wife and three kids – Franklin had just arrived – and I should have been content. I didn't miss the headlines. But I missed boxing. Really missed it.

I had my eye looked at and they told me what I knew but

I didn't want to hear: I had a torn retina. I'd have to get it fixed – and I'd never box again.

It's hard to explain how strong the urge is to fight if you've been doing it all your life. It's part of you. It's the reason you exist. You're born to do it. But it's not for everyone. In fact, it's for very few. It's why you feel special . . . when you're doing it. When you give it up, you leave that special feeling behind. It's just a memory. And there aren't many people who understand how you feel – except other boxers.

I wouldn't pass an eye test so I gave up my boxing licence. It was my university degree, a piece of paper that said who I was, what I did: Frank Bruno, professional boxer. A few months after the Tyson fight, I told the papers I was retiring. I'd have to find other ways to fill the hours in the day. And, in the end, the nights.

People said kind things in the papers. They said I'd proved the critics wrong. Not many of them admitted they were the same people who once reckoned I wasn't good enough. Some of these guys had written me off as far back as the Jumbo Cummings fight. Even Harry Carpenter said my career was finished when Bonecrusher Smith knocked me out.

By the summer of '96, all that was history. All the fights. All the wins. A few defeats. And what did it add up to? Half an hour in a ring a few times a year. Six months as the undisputed heavyweight champion of the world. Now I was about to face a tougher opponent than anyone I'd met in the ring: mental illness.

After I fought Tyson I felt very low. I'd been down before – I always hated losing – but life seemed emptier than ever without the one thing I'd spent my whole career chasing. I didn't know what was wrong. As far as the world was concerned, I was enjoying my retirement, living in a big house in Essex with my family and all that money could buy.

It was the people close to me who noticed it first. I started making plans for family get-togethers, then changing my mind, driving people up the wall. I was spending lots of money for no reason. I bought earth-moving equipment, a thousand pine trees. I was hanging out with strangers and giving my money away. The doctors tell me I thought people were trying to attack me – although I don't remember that. Even at Franklin's christening, I was acting a little strangely – I'd invited the whole world back to our house. My personality was changing. This is when my illness began to affect me. That's what the doctors said. At the time, I didn't notice.

Laura and I were going through personal problems. And the papers got to hear about it. In November 1997, our lawyer Henri Brandman issued a statement saying we having 'difficulties' but that we weren't contemplating divorce. It was tough, but we were hanging in there.

I couldn't sit around the house all day, so I looked at the offers coming in and decided to resume my life on the stage. It was a change of routine – and it was a job. Maybe not a life-threatening job, but something to do.

I reckoned I knew the ropes well enough. I'd worked with Lenny Henry, Michael Barrymore, Cannon and Ball, Frank Carson. So panto it was – *Goldilocks and the Three Bears*, in Birmingham. I had a new business manager, Laurie Mansfield. He wasn't a boxing man but he was big in showbiz, with an agency called International Artistes. So that's the way my career went. We've had our ups and downs, but Laurie's a good man. I'm still with him.

I also took up DJing. Since the day I first heard the choir at my mother's church in Fulham, I've been in love with music – all sorts of music, from Sinatra to Prince. I started at the top with a gig at Hollywood. That's Hollywood, Romford. I was working the deck with three of my nephews, Nigel Hamilton, Andrew Nesbeth and Trevor Rowe. OK, we weren't the Four Tops, but we did all right.

My condition was slowly getting worse, but I couldn't see it. In 1998, my family persuaded me to see a psychiatrist. One minute I was up, the next minute I was down. I was diagnosed with bipolar affective disorder. The doctor prescribed some heavy-duty drugs to calm me.

The diagnosis came as an awful shock. I didn't want to accept it, and I didn't want to be on drugs. This wasn't me. I was one of the fittest guys on the planet. So I stopped taking them. I thought I could beat the illness by myself. It was a stupid thing to do: it made my condition worse. But I didn't know that then.

All I could do was keep busy. For the next four years, my life seemed to centre on panto. Don't get me wrong, I loved it – I loved the audiences, the applause. But maybe I was being typecast. You can only do *Goldilocks* so many times. In '98 we were in Southampton, in '99 it was Woking, Milton Keynes in 2000, Southend the following year. I might never have read a book, but I do know *Goldilocks and the Three Bears* inside out.

And then I tried cocaine. I wish I'd never seen the stuff. It was Las Vegas, 2000, and I was with an old acquaintance and some guys I'd never met before. I think they were high already – and I was a bit wary about them. I bought some coke but I went back to my room alone. That's where it all started.

I took it. Simple as that. I was bored, away from home and I thought, why not? It was like nothing I'd ever taken before. I did it again. And again.

It was nice. Too nice. For six months I was into it. And then I hated it. I loved the buzz it gave me, but I couldn't stand coming down. When I woke up, I felt horrible. It was a sort of deep depression, a black hole with no ending.

This had to stop. Puff I could handle. I understood what it could do. But cocaine was so strong it took control of my brain. And I'd discover it was the worst thing I could be doing with my condition. I was so scared of it, I had to walk away. And I did, quickly. I didn't exactly snort Colombia out of its entire supply.

Most of the time, I kept a low profile – for me. It made a change to wake up and find my face wasn't splashed all over the papers. Then, in 2001, I pulled a stunt that backfired. I can't claim it was my idea – a guy I was doing pantomime with dreamt it up. 'We could do with selling some more tickets, Frank,' he said. 'Why don't you tell the papers you're standing as an MP?' So I did. I really didn't think anyone would believe me: you'd have to be a bit dim to picture me in the House of Commons. Especially when my slogan was 'Don't be a plank, Vote for Frank!'

Everybody fell for it. Even Martin Bell, the former BBC journalist. He was thinking about standing in the same seat, Brentwood and Ongar. 'I like Frank,' he said. 'He's a great guy and he has every right to stand.' This was priceless. Even so, I was feeling a bit guilty: the story had got out of hand. Martin was the man in the white suit; I was the man in fancy dress. What a match-up. I'd only ever voted once in my life, and that was for the Tories after I'd met Margaret Thatcher. I've never been interested in politics.

I reckon the papers knew exactly what was going on. But they printed the story anyway, because they knew it was a headline, that it might sell a few copies. And, yes, a few more tickets to *Goldilocks*.

My world had started to unravel. Laura and I tried to patch up our marriage but it wasn't working. We separated in 2000. Again we had to issue a statement through Henri. We hoped it would persuade the papers to leave us alone for a while. 'It is with great sadness and the deepest regret that we confirm that our relationship has broken down. We will do everything as amicably as possible, and we ask that the media will respect our privacy for the sake of the children. We wish to make it clear that we will make no further comment.'

We'd been together for twenty years. It was a big wrench. A year later we divorced. I don't want to dwell on it because it hurts to drag it up. But we'd grown apart and decided to call it a day. Laura and the kids moved out and I stayed in Stondon Massey. It would be where I went through the most horrible part of my life.

In April 2002 I got a phone call from George Francis's son. George was dead. He'd taken his own life. It was as hard a blow as any I'd had in the ring. I couldn't believe it. Not George. He was as tough as old boots. But it shows we're all vulnerable. He'd had a series of tragedies, one after the other, and he found he couldn't handle it. His wife Joan, whom he'd been with since he was sixteen, died of cancer. Then his youngest son, Simon, died of cancer too. It was too much.

George was a special man, a very caring man. He'd done more than any other trainer to promote black boxers when not many people wanted to know about them. And it was George who persuaded the board to let immigrants fight for British titles. He was there for me in the good times and the bad. He never lost faith in me, unlike a few other people. We were as close as you can get. He had a sign on his wall at home: 'People who take kindness for weakness are the weakest kind of people.' That was George. A gentle philosopher. I miss him every day.

With George and Laura gone, I'd lost two of the most important people in my life. I didn't know who to turn to and I was lonely.

The DJing was a release, a way of forgetting about my troubles, getting out of the house, meeting people. And it was fun. Except the fun was mixed with danger. For days and nights I travelled the motorways on my way to clubs all over the country: Wales, the North, Birmingham, Norwich. You name it, I've probably been there. I made dozens of new friends. Some of them didn't turn out to be too good for me – there are some serious duckers and divers out there. I was falling into bad habits.

Coke wasn't my only nasty experience with drugs. The DJing had put me in a new world. I needed a kick to keep up. I wasn't in control. All I wanted to do was put my troubles in a box and ignore them. But it got worse.

The first time I smoked skunk it nearly blew my head off. It's a dope cocktail that's twenty times stronger than regular puff. The hit went on for hours and I hardly knew who I was or where I was. I couldn't talk, I couldn't walk. I just sat there like a corpse as it ran through my system, screwing up my brain and turning me into a vegetable. It was the most horrible experience.

Skunk was a way to escape, but, down as I was, I knew it was a dumb move. I stopped almost as soon as I started. But stopping didn't make me feel any better. I was now in the grip of mental illness.

It took months to realise what was happening. You try to press on. I was still doing ads, endorsements, telly, but I was under intense pressure. This was worse than anything I'd been through in the ring. I was leading a double life.

I wasn't as reliable as I used to be. I was hard to contact, even for my agent. In May, I was supposed to do a live chat show in Belfast, but I cancelled. Don't know why. I was pretty much out of the picture until August. It's a wonder Laurie didn't give up on me completely.

I was getting used to my new life. I'd left behind my fighting days, the discipline I'd stuck to for sixteen years. And I thought I was having a good time. I was a single man, after all. I had a right to enjoy myself, didn't I? But the reporters were never far away.

I went to an Audley Harrison fight – and that was enough to start another rumour. They said I was making a comeback, that I'd applied for my licence and I wanted to box Audley. It wasn't true, for obvious reasons.

What worries me about these stories is how they upset my kids. I'm hardened to it all, just as I got used to the shenanigans in the fight business. But I don't want my children reading this stuff.

Nothing will stop the papers from printing what they want. But some journalists are better than others. A lot of them have been good friends, including the *Sun*'s boxing man, Colin Hart – and Harry. I can't say I ever had much of a cross word with either of them, or with any of the writers on the boxing beat. It was the rotters I was worried about, the guys who write the 'big' stories up the front of the paper.

But by now I was my own worst enemy. I was hardly sleeping. I was running on pure adrenalin, losing weight and looking awful. Since I was a small boy I had just about lived in the gym. Then, for no reason I can think of, I just stopped. At first I put on weight, ballooning up to about nineteen stone. Then it fell off me. I wasn't eating properly and I was doing a load of puff.

My illness was closing in on me fast. I was confused. So many things were rushing through my mind. And it got really scary. There were celebrities out there I thought were trying to manipulate me. I even believed the Secret Services were out to get me. I'm very patriotic and this upset me terribly.

It was a dreadful time. I couldn't have got through it without the people who loved me. I'd tried the Priory, and I hadn't liked it. But my family wouldn't take no for answer. I was lucky to get into Goodmayes. It's one of the best psychiatric units in the country.

On the day they came to get me my old friend Cass Pennant

was at the house. A lot of my friends had been concerned about me. They didn't want to leave me on my own. I can't tell you how grateful I am to them all.

I wasn't fully aware of it at the time, but the papers – and one in particular – went to town on me after the breakdown. The *Sun*'s 'Bonkers Bruno Locked Up' headline said it all. It was obvious I'd become another disposable celebrity. It was as if all the good times I'd shared with *Sun* readers counted for nothing.

I wasn't naive enough to think it was always going to be roses. I just had no idea how vicious some of the papers could be. I didn't think they'd care so little about the feelings of someone they'd once regarded as a hero. It was obvious I was now just a name that fitted a headline, something that went with 'bonkers'. It was a name people used to cheer. 'Broo-no!' Now I was a national joke.

Every step of the way, reporters have been lurking behind the nearest bush. They say it's the price of fame. But I never wanted to be famous. I just wanted to be a good boxer. I never thought that being good enough to be a champion meant I'd have to give up my privacy, my dignity. I never thought the papers would treat me as a product for ever, something to pick over. I thought it was just a deal we had when I was famous for my boxing – I made the news for them, they sold newspapers, I sold tickets. It seemed simple. But it's never simple. When you sell yourself as a product, there's no buying it back. For better or worse, that's the way it was always going to be, from that St Patrick's Day in 1982 when I knocked out Lupe Guerra, until . . . well, until the day I die.

When I got out of Goodmayes, I had to start all over again. It was up to me now. I couldn't rely on other people to make the really hard choices. I had to face the truth: I was mentally ill.

I wanted people to know I'd come through the storm. In November of 2003, I went to the Royal Variety Performance in Edinburgh. I was stunned and humbled when I got a standing ovation.

The following March, my friends and family put on a tribute lunch for me at the Dorchester hotel in London. Joan had a lot to do with organising that. I don't know what I'd do without her. Michael Watson and Audley Harrison were among the many boxers who turned up. I get a lot of inspiration from Michael. He's such a brave man, capable of many great things still, despite his injuries. You only had to look at him finishing the London Marathon to realise what a special person he is.

Three months later, I was honoured to be part of the British Olympic torch relay that went through London. I was slowly getting back into public life. This is what I was good at, relating to people. The Frank Bruno Show was on the road again.

I did a cruise around the Canaries in December, nothing too taxing – just a few question-and-answer sessions with the passengers. And I've done a bit of television work, too, guesting on *A Question of Sport*, commentating on the boxing with Sky occasionally, and appearing on *Black Icons*, a programme that went out in June 2005.

Last Christmas, Laura and I and the kids went on holiday to Jamaica – Nicola thought it would be a good idea. As usual, the papers made a meal of it. They were on my case again. You had to admire their persistence, I suppose. The photographers had their long lenses on, snapping away all day, waiting for that one picture that would make them rich for a week. I handled it. I knew the truth. I didn't need to read their stories. Just as well.

Nothing I told them could have led them to believe that Laura and I were back together. But that wasn't the story they wanted. They were looking for a fairy tale. I gave them what sounded like a cliché: Laura and I really were just good friends. We had a great couple of weeks. We were on holidays together because the kids wanted us to be. And that's the truth.

It became more bizarre when we got home. I'd been trying to sell the house for a while. I didn't fancy living there any more because it was empty, too full of memories. So I stayed at my sister's and, occasionally, my ex-wife's. It wasn't unusual. At Laura's I got to see the kids on a regular basis, and it was very near to Stondon Massey, so I could help the house sale go through more quickly. It was as simple as that. Not a very exciting story, I know. And not the one that appeared in the papers.

I read that I was begging Laura to take me back, that I was heartbroken when she refused and that I was cracking up again. I couldn't believe they'd write that stuff knowing nothing of the facts. I didn't feel like telling them, either, because, really, it was none of their business. I know that if you're famous people want to read about you, but hadn't they had enough?

Years ago I was famous for being a fighter. Now I was

famous for having been in a mental hospital. But there wasn't anything going on. Why did they have to make it up? Laura and I lead totally different lives, and have done for several years. She has her interests and I have mine. But, as far as the editors were concerned, this was a story that had to have either a happy ending or a very sad one. One way or another, they would get a headline out of it.

Overall, though, life has been so much better than it was. I've sold Stondon Massey, and I've been looking for a new house, something a lot smaller – a mansion and seventy-five acres are no use if there's nobody to share them with. Stephen Purdew, who I met twenty years ago when I was training for the Anders Eklund fight, has let me stay at one of his health farms in the meantime. It's been a great way to chill out while working on this book.

I see the family and they're all growing up nicely. Rachel's going to acting school and Nicola is a freelance beautician. Franklin's still at school, of course. I couldn't ask for better kids.

Laura and I still talk, and we're on good terms – as I keep telling nosy reporters. But they write what they want. This is the truth: I'll always love Laura. Just because you're divorced, it doesn't mean you can't remain close. In fact, it's better between Laura and me now than it has been for a long time. We're friends again. We like to do things with the family. Will we ever get back together? You can never say never in this life, but I don't think so. We've got our own lives to lead. I'm enjoying my little bit of freedom. And, after what I've been through, my freedom means a lot to me.

You can't relive the past. It's just good to be close to the kids and Laura again. I wake up now knowing my nightmare is behind me. I hope and pray it never comes back.

17

Courage

IT TAKES COURAGE TO FIGHT FOR A LIVING IN PUBLIC. AND IT TAKES courage to fight for your sanity in private. I've had to do both – and my second battle has been by far the toughest. If I beat the demons, though, if I stay out of the mental hospital, it will be using the sort of courage I learnt in the boxing ring.

When my father gave me my first pair of gloves, I was hooked on a sport that is unlike any other. It's one on one. And it eats away at you even before you've thrown or taken a punch. What I learnt to do in a boxing ring was beat fear, to conquer my doubts. When I became ill, I had to do the same. Except the fears were far greater. And my opponent was a guy called Frank Bruno.

I might not have been the most naturally gifted boxer, but it was in my blood and I never gave less than 100 per cent. It wasn't easy to climb through the ropes for the first time – or the last, for that matter – but I felt at home in the ring. Boxing was where I belonged. I liked the atmosphere of the gym: the smells, the sounds, the banter, the skipping rope hitting the floor, the guys working the speedball. It was my special place – like it is for all fighters. That's why we understand each other. We know about the pressures of fighting and the sacrifices you have to make even to survive. It's not something you can get your head around unless you've been there.

Putting yourself up for a competitive bout at any level is an act of faith in yourself, in your confidence to deliver what you practise in the gym. You hope you won't bottle it – especially if there are millions of people watching. Boxers don't fear pain – although there can't be many who haven't thought about death or serious injury. What we fear is humiliation. We fear giving up our dignity, our reputation. We fear letting people down, people who put their faith in us. We fear the big L: losing.

Some fighters get used to losing. They decide early on in their careers they're never going to win a world title, or much of anything else except a regular wage. So they settle for being journeymen. But those guys go through the same anxiety champions do. They have the same worries – and the same bills to pay. It's our job. Whatever else it is – torture, sport, entertainment, glory – boxing is a business. As I've said many times, it's show business – with blood.

Some people reckoned I wasn't suited to it, that I lacked a 'killer instinct'. They said I was too nice to be a fighter. Especially a heavyweight. They saw Tyson. Liston. Frazier. They didn't reckon a friendly guy from Wandsworth should be in that sort of game. Appearances can be deceiving, though. I'll be as nice as pie to anyone outside the ring; it's not my way to put people down, to trash-talk. But I knew how to take care of business when the bell went. Ask Mr Coetzee, or Mr McCall. Ask Pierre Coetzer, Jose Ribalta, James Tillis – or any of the forty guys I stopped. Even the guys who beat me – Mike Tyson, Tim Witherspoon, Lennox Lewis, Bonecrusher Smith – I think they'll tell you I gave them something to remember.

When you decide to be a professional boxer, you make a commitment. It's all or nothing. There's no skimping on your training, no running out of the ring, no giving the money back. From my first paid fight to my last, I put everything on the line. In the end, it wasn't my body that suffered as much as my mind. But I don't blame boxing for that – except that I missed it hugely when I had to quit. That did my head in.

I don't think the actual boxing had any effect on my mental condition. I'd had tough fights, but not many. I'd had a lot of early knockout wins, a few easy nights. And I looked after myself. My problems went deeper. They went back further than I knew. They had to do with the person I am.

Since the day seven years ago when the doctors told me I was a manic depressive, I've had to face up to some hard truths. At first I didn't want to believe I was mentally ill. I stopped taking my medicine and I pretended everything would be fine. But I was lying to myself. I know now I'll have to battle with my illness every day for the rest of my life. So far, I'm winning.

It's not a fight you can win alone. You need drugs, you need professional help – and you need your family and friends. I've been lucky to have all three. And most important have been those close to me, the people who saw me falling apart and who persuaded me to get help when I didn't want to. I'd never have done it on my own. And I was lucky too to have friends I didn't even know.

The day I returned to Stondon Massey after my time in Goodmayes, I had the most amazing experience. In the corner of the living room were those huge cardboard boxes. Inside were letters and cards from people all over the world, people who cared about someone whose name they used to shout in boxing halls from London to Las Vegas. I could hardly believe it.

I sat down and started to read some of the letters. I can't tell you what an emotional moment that was. There were thousands and thousands of them – from all parts of the British Isles and Europe, from America, Australia, South Africa, from men, women and kids, many from people who'd suffered from mental illness, or knew someone who had. It made me realise I wasn't alone.

I was surprised how much they understood. They knew about the drugs and the highs and the lows, the terrible desperation, the anxiety, the nervousness. They knew about the loneliness. And they knew about courage.

One man wrote to tell me he'd been diagnosed with bipolar disorder a few years back. He'd eventually come off his medication and gone on to get a degree. 'I have never felt better or more in control of my life,' he said.

Another said he'd been through a divorce, prison and the death of a friend in a short space of time. 'I wish I could hug you and tell you that life gets better,' he said. 'And it will. Believe me.'

There was a letter from one woman which pretty much

summed it up. 'Frank,' she said, 'I know you are in a living hell right now. I know as I, too, have had mental health problems (clinical depression). It is the most bizarre, frightening and lonely feeling in the world. I didn't know what was happening to me, but I do know I would have preferred to have lost a limb than live with the way I was feeling. My heart goes out to you, and I sincerely hope that when that chilling feeling strikes, it doesn't last for long . . . It does get better, Frank, believe me, it does. That hellishly lonely feeling, that is indescribable to anyone unless they have experienced it, will go. Hang on to that belief.'

I tried to answer as many as I could. Annie, who lived across the road, helped me go through them. I'm not a great one for writing letters at the best of times, but I owed it to them. It's amazing what human beings are capable of. We are often at our best when we're cornered.

There was one special message, though. It didn't come through the letter box, but I knew the guy who wrote it would have sent it to me personally if he'd had my address. It appeared in the *Daily Mirror*, a couple of days after I was taken to Goodmayes.

There was so much to take in that I cried. It was a very depressing moment. In our first fight he was as good a boxer as I ever met. But he has obviously had some really tough battles outside the ring which have done him in. I had no idea things were that bad. Frank should not be cast away like some used cloth. He's better than that and I know the British people will see him right. It's not like Frank was punch-drunk from being beaten up for so many years like some boxers. He pretty much held his own. I always thought he did a great job walking away from boxing when he did. He got a good title and got a good pay day. But for us boxers fighting is just a way of making a living. That's the easy part. The hard part is making a life outside.

It was from Mike Tyson.

I would never claim I've had it harder than others. There are people who are starving, being shot at, all sorts of terrible things. I was once heavyweight champion of the world. I couldn't ask for more than that. It's what I wanted. How many people are lucky enough to get what they want in life?

But I've come through my own sort of hell too. I looked into an awful place inside my mind and, somehow, handled it. Maybe my story will give hope to other people with similar problems. I'd like to think so.

What next for me? When I retired from boxing in 1996, I wondered where my life was going. Nine years later, I think I know. I'm chilling out, doing the odd bit of work here and there. I've even done some training – with Wayne Rooney's brother, Graham. He's not bad, either. I don't know if I'll get into that full-time but I do know I'm back in the Bruno business. I've kept my sense of humour and I always reckon there's good stuff around the corner.

The most important thing in my life is not panto or playing records in nightclubs or going on television. All of that's fun, but it means nothing without my family. I still have them – or, at least, the kids – and I'm getting on better with Laura now than I have done for a long time. I wake up each day and the world seems fine.

I'll take lithium for as long as I have to. I'd love to come off it; if I continue to improve over the next few years, the doctors might even let me do that. But that won't be my decision. I have to trust the experts. I learnt that when I stopped taking my drugs seven years ago.

My life has always been full of twists and turns, and I don't suppose the future will be any different. Like everyone else's life. Mine just happens to be lived out in the newspapers, on television. And in this book. It's the story so far.

What happened to me in 2003 scared the wits out of me; I never want to go through that again – which is why I'm determined to stick to my new lifestyle. That means good food, regular exercise and keeping an eye on my mood swings. I have them under control most of the time, although we all snap occasionally.

What keeps me dedicated to my new life is the memory of the old one. I have a lot of respect for the people who work in Pathways clinic. Without them, I might not be here at all. But I can't imagine going back to hospital. It's not the place – it's being locked up. That's too frightening to even think about. I've confronted my illness but I'm not sure what I'd do if I broke down again and they took me away. I might even do a runner. I'm serious. I know it would be stupid but that's how much I value my freedom. But that was then. I'm living for today and tomorrow, and I'm doing everything I can to make sure I stay well.

If there is a secret to controlling my moods I think I've found it in the gym. When I'm working out, I'm on a natural high. I feel good about myself and about others. I'd like to get down to sixteen and a half stone – which was near to my best fighting weight – so I work out nearly every day. I eat sensibly and then I burn off the calories.

When I gave up training my weight fluctuated. I'd either be skinny or fat. Blowing up to about nineteen stone three years ago felt awful. I didn't like myself. I was angry at the world and I just stopped training. That was the time when my world fell to bits and it can't have been a coincidence that I'd let myself go. Then I lost loads of weight. I wasn't in control of my body.

Sometimes when I stop working out I get a bit snappy with people. A bit aggressive. It's not nice. I know it. That's why I keep training. Probably, I will never be able to stop. I was a prisoner of the gym when I was boxing; and I still am.

When George committed suicide I was as low as I'd ever been. But I never thought about ending my own life. Whatever my problems, I haven't forgotten how to laugh. Sometimes, living on my own, I get a bit lonely; you can wonder what it's all about if there's no special somebody to come home to. It also takes a while for me to trust anyone – I'm a bit cynical, I guess – and that makes forming any relationship difficult. But that's the way it goes. I've got to live with who I am.

Most days, I'm happy. I'm so much better than I was two years ago. I'm so much better than I was nine years ago too, the night I lost my title, my career and my reason for getting up in the morning. I can look back now – and I sometimes do, like all fighters – at my fights, the good nights and the bad. Some nights were so beautiful, the perfect punch, the thrill of winning.

There were so many highs but you knew there would be a

low moment not far away. And I think it's the same for many boxers. They're complicated human beings. I might be wrong, but I think some of them aren't that happy. They're addicts – hooked on the special thrill of fighting. And they know that one day it will end. I hated having to give boxing up – but, in a way, it was a blessing. It stopped me carrying on too long. My eye injury saved me from fighting past my best.

There's no question boxing is a drug. My old mate Charlie Magri used to say that. And I fear for the older guys who are still in the game, who fight on when maybe they don't need to, great fighters like Evander Holyfield and Riddick Bowe, for instance. They've got plenty of money – but they can't buy the thrill of the big fight. I think they do it to satisfy their ego, to hear the crowd. They can't let it go. It gives them a purpose, I suppose. I can't really argue with that. It's up to them.

Oliver McCall, the man I beat to win the title, is still fighting. Good luck to him. I'm glad it's not me in there. Twelve rounds with the Atomic Bull was quite enough. Oliver's a rough diamond, but I like him. I just hope he doesn't end up a mess, because he's had one tough life in and out of the ring.

The fighter I will always be linked to looks like he's finally called it a day. I hope so. Mike Tyson has had more than his share of troubles.

In June 2005, Mike had his last fight. It wasn't the Tyson I fought twice. It was a 38-year-old man who had nothing left except his name. Towards the end of the sixth round against a big Irishman called Kevin McBride, Mike was pushed backwards and fell to the canvas. He just sat there, lying against the ropes. He didn't look that hurt. But you could see the pain in his eyes. You could see he didn't want to get up. When he did, he wandered back to the stool in his corner, sat down and quit.

Later, he said something that only Mike could say. 'I'm a cold and a cruel and a hard person. I've been around the worst. You can't take away what's happened to me. I've been abused any way anyone can be abused. I'm not used to sensitivity any more. Don't cry. I don't know how to handle people crying any more. I've lost my sensitivity.' It was the saddest thing I'd ever heard.

Whatever's happened to me – good and bad – I'd do it all again. I love my family, I've made a good living and I'm beating my illness. But it's boxing that made me who I am. It might not be the nicest business in the world but it was my business. It's the only one I knew. And as long as I live I have a moment to remember. The moment the ring announcer told the world I was the heavyweight champion of the world.

Acknowledgements

I would like to thank many people – and apologies if I've left anyone out: Annie and Jim from across the road, who helped me answer the many thousands of letters I've received; Vera, who looked after my dogs at the kennels; my sister Joan, who has been a rock in bad times and good; the rest of my family, who have been great too; my old friend Bert Hamilton; Cass Pennant, who was there from the start; 'Big Dave' Carroll, who was always there; Colin Smith, who looked after Stondon Court and became a good friend; Terry and Mickey, who were part of the adventure, and Frank Warren too; Phipps, who always makes me laugh; Stafford Cox and Keith Morton, who did so much to get me into shape during my career; Stephen Purdew, who has been a generous host for a long time; my agent Laurie Mansfield; Eugenie Furniss at William Morris; all the people at Yellow Jersey; my co-author Kevin. And two other sets of people: all the boxers I fought, even the ones who beat me; and to the staff at Pathways clinic at Goodmayes hospital, who helped me get through the toughest fight of my life.

The author and publishers would like to make grateful acknowledgement to the following for permission to reproduce photographs:

Empics for the fight against Rudi Pika (*p. ii*), against 'Jumbo' Cummings (*p. iii*), inset picture with Mike Tyson (*p. v*), handing a writ to Lennox Lewis (*p. vii*), the Tom Jenkins portrait (*p. ix*), against Oliver McCall (*p. x*), with Laura and Nicola (*p. xi*), the bus tour of London (*p. xi*), on a break from Goodmayes (*inset*) (*p. xiv*), and with Russell Crowe (*p. xv*); Popperfoto for the portrait of Frank with Terry Lawless (*p. ii*), against 'Bonecrusher' Smith (*p. iii*), against Gerrie Coetzee (*p. iv*), against Tim Witherspoon (*p. iv*), working the speedball in Canning Town (*p. vi*), against Lewis (*p. vii*), with Laura after the Lewis fight (*p. viii*), with George Francis (*p. ix*), and Laura (*p. xii*); Magnum Photos for the portrait of Frank with his mother (*p. ii*); London Features International for the portrait of Frank and Harry Carpenter (*p. iii*), Frank and Laura on their wedding day (*p. viii*), Frank on his way to the ring (*p. xii*), DJing with his nephews (*p. xiv*), with Sooty (*p. xiv*), and opening the Bellingdon and Asheridge fête (*p. xv*); Offside for the '89 fight against Mike Tyson (*p. v*), against Jose Ribalta (*p. vii*), and against Tyson in '96 (*p. xvi*); Action Images for the portrait of Frank and

Mickey Duff (*p. vi*), Mike Tyson and Don King (*p. xii*), and against Tyson in '96 (*p. xiii*); the BBC for Frank as Juliet (*p. vi*); Rex Images for the portrait of Frank with Franklin Jr (*p. xi*), and on a break from Goodmayes (*p. xiv*); Harry Borden for the portrait of Frank (*p. xvi*).

Every effort has been made to trace or contact all copyright holders. The publishers will be pleased to correct any omissions brought to their notice at the earliest opportunity.

The mental health charity SANE provides a helpline for all mental health problems. Staffed by trained volunteers, SANELINE is open every day of the year. The SANELINE number is 0845 767 8000.

Professional Record of Frank Bruno

All venues in London, unless otherwise stated

Date	Opponent	Venue	Result
1982			
17 March	Lupe Guerra	Royal Albert Hall	Won KO 1
20 March	Harvey Steichen	Wembley Arena	Won RSC 2
20 April	Tom Stevenson (*later*	Royal Albert Hall	Won KO 1
	Abdul Mahaymin)		
4 May	Ronald Gibbs	Wembley Arena	Won RSC 4
1 June	Tony Moore	Royal Albert Hall	Won RSC 2
14 September	George Scott	Wembley Arena	Won RSC 1
23 October	Ali Lukasa	Berlin	Won KO 2
9 November	Rudy Gauwe	Royal Albert Hall	Won KO 2
24 November	George Butzbach	Royal Albert Hall	Won RSC 1
7 December	Gilberto Acuna	Royal Albert Hall	Won RSC 1
1983			
18 January	Stewart Lithgo	Royal Albert Hall	Won RSC 4
8 February	Peter Mulindwa	Royal Albert Hall	Won KO 3
1 March	Winston Allen	Royal Albert Hall	Won RSC 2
5 April	Eddie Neilson	Royal Albert Hall	Won RSC 3
3 May	Scott LeDoux	Wembley Arena	Won RSC 3
31 May	Barry Funches	Royal Albert Hall	Won RSC 5
9 July	Mike Jameson	DiVinci Manor, Chicago	Won KO 2
27 September	Bill Sharkey	Wembley Arena	Won KO 1
11 October	Floyd 'Jumbo'	Royal Albert Hall	Won RSC 7
	Cummings		
6 December	Walter Santemore	Royal Albert Hall	Won KO 4
1984			
13 March	Juan Figueroa	Wembley Arena	Won KO 1
13 May	James 'Bonecrusher'	Wembley Arena	Lost KO 10
	Smith		

25 September	Ken Lakusta	Wembley Arena	Won KO 2
6 November	Jeff Jordan	Royal Albert Hall	Won RSC 3
27 November	Phil Brown	Wembley Arena	Won PTS 10

1985

26 March	Lucien Rodriguez	Wembley Arena	Won RSC 1
1 October	Anders Eklund	Wembley Arena	Won KO 4
4 December	Larry Frazier	Royal Albert Hall	Won KO 2

1986

4 March	Gerrie Coetzee	Wembley Arena	Won RSC 1
19 July	Tim Witherspoon	Wembley Stadium	Lost RSC 11

1987

24 March	James Tillis	Wembley Arena	Won RSC 5
27 June	Chuck Gardner	Cannes	Won KO 1
30 August	Reggie Gross	Nueva Andalucia Bullring, Marbella	Won RSC 8
24 October	Joe Bugner	White Hart Lane	Won RSC 8

1989

25 February	Mike Tyson	Hilton Hotel, Las Vegas	Lost RSC 5

1991

20 November	John Emmen	Royal Albert Hall	Won KO 1

1992

22 April	Jose Ribalta	Wembley Arena	Won KO 2
17 October	Pierre Coetzer	Wembley Arena	Won RSC 8

1993

24 April	Carl Williams	National Exhibition Centre, Birmingham	Won RSC 10
1 October	Lennox Lewis	Arms Park, Cardiff	Lost RSC 7

1994

| 16 March | Jesse Ferguson | National Exhibition Centre, Birmingham | Won RSC 1 |

1995

18 February	Rodolfo Marin	Bath & West Country Showground, Shepton Mallet	Won RSC 1
13 May	Mike Evans	Kelvin Hall, Glasgow	Won KO 2
2 September	Oliver McCall	Wembley Stadium	Won PTS 12

1996

| 16 March | Mike Tyson | MGM Grand, Las Vegas | Lost RSC 3 |

Record: 40 wins (38 by stoppage), 5 defeats

KO: Knockout
RSC: Referee stopped contest
PTS: Points

3 1143 00745 2742